SPARKNOTES
101

U.S. History
Colonial Period through 1865

SPARK PUBLISHING

SPARKNOTES is a registered trademark of SparkNotes LLC

Spark Educational Publishing
A Division of Barnes & Noble Publishing
120 Fifth Avenue
New York, NY 10011
www.sparknotes.com

ISBN 1-4114-0335-5

Please submit changes or report errors to
www.sparknotes.com/errors

Printed and bound in the United States.

Library of Congress Cataloging-in-Publication Data

SparkNotes 101 U.S. history.
    v. cm.
  Includes bibliographical references and index.
  Contents: [1] From the precolonial period to 1865 -- [2] 1865 to
    modern times.
  ISBN 1-4114-0335-5 (v. 1) -- ISBN 1-4114-0336-3 (v. 2)
  1. United States--History--Outlines, syllabi, etc. 2. United States
    --History--Examinations--Study guides. I. Title: SparkNotes
    101 United States history. II. Title: SparkNotes one hundred
    one U.S. history. III. Title: SparkNotes one hundred and one
    U.S. history.
  E178.2.S695 2005
  973--dc22
                    2005009726

Contents

Acknowledgments

SparkNotes would like to thank the following writers and contributors:

Kelly McMichael-Stott, Ph.D.
Professor of History, Texas Christian University

Gregg Cantrell, Ph.D.
Professor of History and Erma and Ralph Lowe Chair in Texas History, Texas Christian University

Ashley Laumen
Teaching Assistant, Department of History, Texas Christian University

Josh Cracaft
A.B., Government, Harvard University

Andrew Jones
B.A., International Studies, Oglethorpe University; M.A., Slavic Languages and Literature, Ohio State University; M.S., Journalism, Boston University

Anaxos, Inc.

A Note from SparkNotes

Welcome to the *SparkNotes 101* series! This book will help you succeed in your introductory college course for U.S. History: Colonial Period through 1865.

Every component of this study guide has been designed to help you process the course material more quickly and score higher on your exams. You'll see lots of headings, lists, charts, maps, and, most important, no long blocks of text. This format will allow you to quickly situate yourself and easily get to the crux of your course. We've organized the book in the following manner:

Introduction: Before diving in to the major chapters, this short introduction will present a broader view of the themes that will be covered in more detail later on. Remember, it is these over-arching themes that are usually tested on exams.

Chapters 1–9: Each chapter provides a clarification of material included in your textbook. Key features include:

- **Sidebars:** Throughout the text, these call out main points and relate material to major themes.

- **Key Terms:** Important names, events, amendments, treaties, etc., are bolded throughout each chapter for quick scanning and reviewing.

- **A+ Student Essay:** It's the real thing. Each chapter contains a typical essay prompt with a response that will show you how to pull together the facts from the chapter and use them in a compelling argument. At the same time, these essays delve more deeply into particular topics in history, enriching the content of each chapter.

- **Sample Test Questions:** These show you the kind of questions you are most likely to encounter on a test. Bulleted points follow each question and clarify the kind of information you need to include in your answers.

- **Timeline:** This end-of-chapter outline provides an at-a-glance recap of major events.

- **Major Figures:** This section provides a summary of the major figures presented in the chapter, along with their significance.

- **Suggested Reading:** This list makes recommendations for enhancing your knowledge with further research in notable books.

Index: Use the index at the back of the book to make navigation easier or to look up specific events, people, documents, treaties, and other topics.

We hope *SparkNotes 101: U.S. History: Colonial Period through 1865* helps you, gives you confidence, and occasionally saves your butt! Your input makes us better. Let us know what you think or how we can improve this book at **www.sparknotes.com/comments**.

Introduction

Several themes or key ideas emerge when we look at the broad sweep of American history from the Colonial Period through 1865. These major themes include:

- The Struggle to Define American Citizenship

- The Exclusion of Nonwhites from American Society

- The Westward Expansion of America

- The Development of a National Economy

- The Struggle to Define the Role of Government

- The Emergence of a National Culture

- The Belief in American Exceptionalism

The Struggle to Define American Citizenship

The Declaration of Independence proclaims that "all men are created equal, that they are endowed by their Creator with certain unalienable rights, that among these are life, liberty, and the pursuit of happiness." One of the most significant pursuits of the American people was to define more specifically what rights American citizens should enjoy and exactly who gets to enjoy them. The struggle to define American citizenship includes the following important trends:

- **The expansion of the voting class from 1776 through the 1820s.** The rise in the number of white men who voted in elections during this time period is often referred to as Jacksonian Democracy, even though this increase in citizen participation began prior to Andrew Jackson's terms as president.

- **The changing position of African Americans in American society.** The struggle to define the social and legal status of African Americans began well before Independence.

1

The Constitution originally institutionalized slavery, but Americans became increasingly conflicted about the legitimacy of this institution. This question was finally decided by the Civil War. Legislation resulting from the war ended slavery, and the Fourteenth Amendment to the Constitution guaranteed African Americans important rights of citizenship, such as the right to vote.

- **The changing position of women in American society.** The Fourteenth Amendment, which established the rights of freedmen, did not apply to women, and women did not gain the right to vote until fifty-two years after its passage. However, American women struggled throughout this period to gain suffrage, and even longer to gain economic and social equality.

The Exclusion of Nonwhites from American Society

Even as Americans sought to define citizenship and its privileges, the belief in the racial superiority of whites was prevalent and nonwhites were excluded and marginalized from society. Examples of this exclusion include:

- **The displacement of Native Americans.** Native Americans were pushed continually westward throughout the early history of the United States, with the most dramatic instance being the forced removal of the Five Civilized Tribes in the 1830s under Andrew Jackson's Indian Removal Act. When Native Americans and white Americans did coexist, white Americans demanded that Native Americans assimilate and forfeit their own cultures, languages, religion, and dress.

- **The increasingly harsh treatment of African Americans.** Slavery continued until the Civil War, and as opposition to the war grew, the mistreatment of African Americans intensified. African Americans were increasingly stripped of social, political, and legal rights. America explicitly defined African American slaves as property with the Dred Scott Supreme Court case of 1857.

The Westward Expansion of America

The theme of westward expansion is central to the first half of American history. Expansion was a major driving force, bringing Europeans to the Americas and eventually enlarging the United States until it stretched from ocean to ocean and beyond. The belief that America has a right, a duty, and a destiny to expand is referred to as Manifest Destiny. Significant episodes of westward expansion during this period include:

- **The move across the Allegheny Mountains** by colonists in the eighteenth century.

- **The acquisition of the Louisiana Territory** from France in 1803.

- **The Texas Revolution and the Mexican-American War**, in which American settlers revolted from the Mexican government and eventually applied for statehood.

- **The opening of the West** to pioneers by covered wagon.

- **The gold rush of 1849**, which lured thousands of settlers, hoping to strike it rich, to California.

The Development of a National Economy

The United States committed itself to enlarging and promoting its own economy in the Constitution, creating a system conducive to internal economic improvements. Although not all citizens agreed on how the national economy should be organized and regulated, Americans as a whole wanted a robust economy that promoted their business interests. Examples of efforts to reshape the national economy include:

- **Alexander Hamilton's financial reforms**, including the creation of a National Bank

- **Henry Clay's American System**, including a high protective tariff to stimulate national growth

- **Struggles over protective tariffs of goods**, which benefited the South and West but not the industrial Northeast

- **Struggles over the continuance and expansion of slavery into new territories**, including the Compromise of 1820, the Missouri Compromise, and the Bleeding Kansas incident

The Struggle to Define the Role of Government

When the colonists declared their independence, the new government enjoyed a consensus among its leaders, but that consensus changed quickly to disagreement, particularly in regard to what form the government should take.

The Federalists, led by Alexander Hamilton, fought to ratify the Constitution even though a significant portion of the population wanted to continue under the Articles of Confederation. The Constitution created a stronger central government in order to increase the nation's economic power.

By 1800, American politics had developed into an antagonism between two definite and competing political parties. The Federalists (the heirs of Hamilton's party) supported a strong federal government that encouraged manufacturing and commercial interests, while the Democratic-Republicans (also known simply as the Republicans) promoted a more democratically aligned and looser government suited to an agriculturally based nation.

Some of the confrontations during this period include:

- **The controversy over the Alien and Sedition Acts.** The Federalists enacted laws to silence their political opposition, and two leading Republicans, James Madison and Thomas Jefferson, responded by issuing the Kentucky and Virginia Resolutions, arguing that the Alien and Sedition Acts violated the First Amendment and the rights of the states.

- **The Bank War and Tariff crisis** that occurred during Andrew Jackson's presidency during the 1830s, which reinvigorated the argument about the powers of the federal government relative to those of the states.

- **The Nullification Crisis** under Jackson, which posed questions such as whether power should reside with the federal or state governments and how the power and responsibilities of each should be distributed.

- **The debate about slavery,** which intensified the conflicts between the states and the federal government. Beginning with the Compromise of 1820, through the Missouri Compromise, and ending with the Civil War, political leaders wrestled with whether the government should protect or abolish slavery.

The Emergence of a National Culture

The creation of a cohesive national identity from the diverse array of peoples in America proved a challenge to the young nation. Some examples of the emerging national culture include:

- **Hector St. John de Crèvecoeur's *Letters from an American Farmer*,** the first description of the blurring of national and religious differences that occurred in the middle colonies. De Crèvecoeur maintained that the merging represented a "new race" of people.

- **The creation of a historical story,** including the tale of Paul Revere that warned the residents of Lexington and Concord the British were coming; Washington's crossing the Delaware; and the eventual adoption of Francis Scott Key's "The Star Spangled Banner," a poem detailing the British bombardment of Fort McHenry on September 13, 1814, as the national anthem.

- **Transcendentalism,** representing the emergence of a distinctively American school of philosophy and literature.

- **A uniquely American poetic voice**, such as Walt Whitman and Emily Dickinson.

The Belief in American Exceptionalism

American exceptionalism is the belief that the American people and government hold a unique and extraordinary position in the world because of America's adherence to democratic principles based upon personal and economic freedom.

Historians discredit the idea of American exceptionalism now, but Americans held the notion in high regard during the period prior to 1865. Some Americans at that time interpreted it to mean a sort of moral superiority. Dissenters argued that the ideals of exceptionalism represented little more than propaganda or a justification for an American-centered view of the world.

Examples of belief in an American exceptionalism before 1865 include:

- **America as a new world**, redeeming the old and sparking a renaissance in ideas, government, and wealth.

- **John Winthrop's "City upon a Hill" sermon**, which urged Americans to see themselves as creating a model society for the rest of the world to follow.

- **The lessening of social constraints and conventions** that offered opportunities, or at least the hope of opportunities, to a larger number of people.

- **The belief that the United States was founded on a set of ideals rather than a common heritage.** In the words of Abraham Lincoln in his Gettysburg Address, America was "conceived in liberty, and dedicated to the proposition that all men are created equal."

- **The federalist system of government with checks and balances**, allowing a greater diversity of local control and

enabling citizens to determine laws for their own locales. No "tyranny of the majority" ruled the nation.

- **The prevalence of religious toleration**, and the federal government seeking a definite split between the church and the state.

- **Particular civil rights granted to all citizens**, including the right to free speech, to assemble freely, and to bear arms.

- **The concept of Manifest Destiny**, or the belief that the United States was divinely ordained to inhabit the continent from the Atlantic to the Pacific Ocean.

Colliding Cultures: Pre–Columbian Period to 1700

- Pre–Columbian America
- Early European Exploration
- English Dominance in North America

Columbus's return from his 1492 voyage to the New World sparked an era of exploration throughout Europe. Explorers and settlers traveled to the New World for many reasons. The Spaniards and Portuguese who first arrived in the fifteenth and sixteenth centuries mainly sought to make their fortune. These explorers conquered the natives and plundered ancient cities in search of riches. Later, most settlers came to the New World to seek a new beginning, with the freedom to worship and live as they pleased.

Within 200 years of Columbus's initial discovery, Spain, Portugal, France, England, and the Netherlands had all established colonies and vied for dominance in the Western Hemisphere. Spain eventually gained control of most of Central and South America, while Britain dominated North America. American colonists in British North America enjoyed a relative degree of political autonomy and later grew resentful of Britain's attempts to exert more control.

Pre-Columbian America

About 12,000 years ago, bands of hunters from northeast Asia pursued mammoths and other big game across a frozen patch of land known as **Beringia**, unwittingly becoming the first Americans. This land bridge has since disappeared and become the salty **Bering Strait** that divides Siberia from Alaska. Cold weather and harsh conditions drove these hunters south in search of food and a better climate. Gradually, they spread across North and South America and formed various Native American tribes. Historians have learned about these people from the artifacts they left behind, including stone tools and weapons, bones, pottery, ancient dwellings, and bits of textiles and basketry.

Though most historians believe the first Americans arrived from Asia, debate rages among anthropologists and archeologists about how and when the first Americans arrived. Archeological evidence found in 1927 indicated that the first known natives arrived around 12,000 years ago, and no one questioned this evidence for more than fifty years. Since 1980, however, discoveries made at several archeological sites have proven that people lived in the Americas much earlier than 12,000 years ago. These new findings have created a stir in the archeological community.

CENTRAL AND SOUTH AMERICAN NATIVES

By the time Christopher Columbus first set eyes on the New World, more than 50 million people lived in North and South America. About 4 million of those people lived in what is now the United States. The richest, most complex native civilizations developed near the **Isthmus of Panama**, the thin strip of land that divides North and South America. There were four major civilizations in this area:

- **The Mayas**, who lived just north of the Isthmus of Panama, developed a sophisticated approach to mathematics and astronomy and a calendar more accurate than that of Europe.

- **The Toltecs**, who lived in the center of present-day Mexico, had conquered most of Central America by the tenth century.

- **The Aztecs**, who frequently made ritual human sacrifices, founded **Tenochtitlán** in 1325, now known as Mexico City.

- **The Incas**, or **Quechua** people, who inhabited the Andes Mountains, developed elaborate road systems and a strong central government.

These four civilizations distinguished themselves from other Native American societies in South America. They are considered more advanced civilizations for the following accomplishments:

- Establishing permanent cities

- Developing large-scale agricultural techniques to raise such crops as maize (corn), beans, squash, chili peppers, avocados, and pumpkins

- Building giant pyramids, courts for ceremonial games, and other monumental architecture

- Engaging in complex commercial and military practices

NORTH AMERICAN NATIVES

In North America, three distinct native civilizations emerged:

- **The Adena-Hopewell** culture of the Northeast, which had reached its peak by the seventh century, long before European conquest. European settlers later encountered their distant descendants in the **Iroquois** and **Pequot** tribes.

- **The Mississippian** culture of the Southeast, which developed sophisticated agricultural practices and created temple mounds akin to the pyramids built in South America. The Mississippians thrived until the fifteenth century, when European diseases wiped them out. The **Creeks**, **Cherokees**, **Choctaw**, **Chickasaws**, and **Seminoles** all descend from this culture.

- **The Pueblo-Hohokam** people of the Southwest, who developed elaborate irrigation systems. Their descendants include the **Hopi**, **Zuni**, and **Anasazi** tribes.

None of these native cultures developed to the same degree of sophistication as the Mayas, Aztecs, or Incas. However, most of the native peoples in North America were able to maintain large agricultural systems, as well as build ceremonial mounds or pueblo dwellings, and develop elaborate clan structures.

Early European Exploration

During the fourteenth, fifteenth, and sixteenth centuries, Europe underwent a period of fast-paced change and development known as the **Renaissance**, meaning "rebirth." Rampant disease, political fragmentation, and religious hysteria had plagued Europeans throughout the medieval period between the fifth and the thirteenth centuries. The Renaissance, however, featured:

- The revival of learning, with emphasis placed on ancient Greek and Roman scholarship

- The growth of major European cities

- The development of trade and capitalistic economies

- The rise of new and powerful monarchies

Increased power and wealth in the hands of the monarchies eventually led to an interest in exploration and expansion.

> *Johann Gutenberg's invention of the movable-type printing press in 1440 made books and knowledge accessible on a scale never before known. The widespread availability of affordable books on various subjects helped fuel the Renaissance, when people began to question their beliefs about the world around them.*

COLUMBUS'S VOYAGES

Italian-born **Christopher Columbus** learned to sail from Portuguese seamen. After years of sailing on Portuguese ships, Columbus hatched his own plan to lead an expedition westward in the hopes of finding a faster route to Asia across the Atlantic. He eventually received financial backing from King Ferdinand

and Queen Isabella of Spain in exchange for the gold, spices, and silk he promised to bring back from the Orient.

The Voyage of 1492

Columbus and eighty-seven other men set sail aboard three ships: the *Nina, Pinta,* and *Santa Maria.* After a rocky thirty-three-day voyage, they landed on an island in the Bahamas. They named it **San Salvador.** Columbus called the friendly island people *los indios* (Indians) because he believed he and his men had landed on an island in the East Indies.

Columbus then sailed southward down to Cuba and to the island of **Hispaniola** in search of the mainland. When one of his ships sank, he decided to return home. Leaving forty men behind, Columbus seized a dozen natives to give to the King and Queen of Spain and sailed back across the Atlantic.

> *Contrary to popular belief,* **Vikings** *actually discovered the New World before Columbus. They colonized Iceland, Greenland, and Newfoundland in the ninth and tenth centuries and then began exploring the eastern coast of Canada. Archeological findings have confirmed oral historical accounts of their early discovery of North America. The Vikings had withdrawn from their colonies by the eleventh century, and the details of their early explorations remained unknown to later European explorers.*

Columbus's Return Trips to America

Columbus returned to Spain a hero and prepared for a second voyage. He sailed back to the Americas in 1493 with seventeen ships, more than 1,200 men, and instructions from the king and queen to treat the Indians well. Unfortunately, the forty men Columbus had left on Hispaniola after his first voyage had raped and murdered many Indians and had plundered their villages. The natives had struck back in return and killed ten Spaniards. Columbus counterattacked with crossbows and guns and loaded five hundred natives on a ship bound for the slave markets in Spain. He made two more voyages to the Caribbean in the next decade but refused to believe he had discovered anything other than outlying parts of Asia.

*Sixteenth-century mapmaker Martin Waldseemueller published the first map of the New World in 1507. He named the continents "Americas" to honor Italian explorer **Amerigo Vespucci**, who first sailed near the mainland of America in 1499. Vespucci amazed Europeans with a published account of his voyages in 1504, in which he claimed to have discovered an entirely new continent.*

SPANISH EXPLORATION

By the early sixteenth century, Spain had begun an inland conquest of the Americas mainly to search for gold, silver, and other riches. Spanish conquistadors, or "conquerors," penetrated much of present-day Latin America and established a vast new-world empire for Spain by the 1530s. The following men were the most famous of these conquistadors:

- **Hernando Cortés**, who conquered the Aztecs at Tenochtitlán with only 600 men in 1519

- **Francisco Pizarro**, who defeated the Incas in 1532

- **Hernando De Soto**, who explored the present-day southwestern United States with 600 men in 1539

"Biological Exchange"

An enormously influential exchange occurred when the Europeans landed in the Americas, generally to the benefit of Europeans and detriment of the native peoples. Sugar and bananas crossed the Atlantic, while pigs, sheep, and cattle arrived in the Americas. However, European diseases such as influenza, typhus, measles, and smallpox also crossed the Atlantic and devastated the Native American population.

Subjugation of the Native Americans

The Spanish explored all of South and Central America and eventually became the privileged landowners of the newly discovered continent. They created the *encomienda* system, in which favored Spanish officers controlled land and the nearby native villages.

These officers protected the villages but also demanded tributes from the natives in the form of goods and labor.

Not surprisingly, a bipolar society emerged in Spanish America, with affluent Europeans at the top and poor, subjugated natives at the bottom. By the mid-1500s, much of the Native American population had died from disease, guns, or overwork. To replace this labor force, the Spanish began importing slaves from Africa.

CHALLENGES TO SPAIN'S EMPIRE

Spain also dominated much of southern and western North America during the colonial period, but not without serious competition from the French, the Dutch, and the English. The French challenged Spanish claims first, most significantly when explorer **Jacques Cartier** made three voyages into present-day Canada in the 1530s. Religious civil wars in France halted further attempts to colonize North America until **Samuel de Champlain** founded "New France," a territory that covered much of eastern Canada in the 1600s.

Spain also suffered from Dutch and English pirates who plundered Spanish ships as they crisscrossed the Atlantic. War eventually erupted between Spain and England in the mid-1500s, ending with England's defeat of the Spanish Armada in 1588. The defeat of the armada marked the beginning of British naval supremacy and opened the way for English colonization of the New World.

*Historians refer to this time as the **Age of Exploration**, but it has also become known as the **Age of Exploitation** or the **Age of Conquest**. The terms imply different ways of looking at the period and illustrate differences among the historians who use them.*

English Dominance in North America

Early English attempts at colonization proved unsuccessful and expensive, but colonists soon managed to establish themselves in the wilderness of North America. By the eighteenth century, England had replaced Spain as the dominant colonial power on the continent.

THE COLONIZATION MOVEMENT

Several factors made the acquisition of New-World colonies a virtual necessity for England:

- Spanish gold and silver from the New World had flooded Europe and created a severely inflated economy.

- England did not have any colonies that produced gold and therefore suffered greatly from the inflation.

- English farmers had begun growing foods in the Americas, such as corn and potatoes, which helped to eliminate starvation but contributed to the population boom.

- The increased population combined with extreme inflation fueled the unemployment rate in England.

With a depressed economy, high unemployment rates, and grow-ing populations, England needed somewhere to send its citizens to discover riches and relieve the cities of their unemployed masses.

"THE LOST COLONISTS"

In 1578, Queen Elizabeth I granted Sir Humphrey Gilbert a royal patent to explore and claim new territories in North America. Gilbert hoped to transplant Britons to the Americas to acquire wealth for himself and for England. On his first voyage in 1583, he managed to claim some land in Newfoundland but had to turn back as winter approached. Tragically, he and his ship van-ished on the return trip.

The next year, Gilbert's half-brother **Sir Walter Raleigh** petitioned the queen for a commission in his own name. In 1587,
Raleigh sponsored an expedition of 117 men, women, and children, who settled on Roanoke Island off the coast of North Carolina. The Spanish–English War prevented any further ships from
sailing to **Roanoke**, and three years passed before another
English ship arrived in 1590. Strangely, the sailors found the settlement abandoned. To this day, historians do not know what
happened to those "Lost Colonists."

MANAGING THE COSTS OF COLONIZATION

New-World colonization soon became so expensive that no single individual could fund expeditions. Instead, English entrepreneurs formed **joint-stock companies** in which stockholders
shared the risks and profits of colonization. These stockholders
expected to earn a return on their investments in the form of
gold and silver, wines, citrus fruits, olive oil, and other spoils that
would result from colonization. Some of the larger companies
such as the **Virginia Company** acquired patents from the monarchy and held monopolies on large tracts of land.

JAMESTOWN

In 1607, three ships carrying almost 100 men reached the Chesapeake Bay. These settlers chose a highly defensible site along the
James River in present-day Virginia and established the small settlement of **Jamestown**.

First Encounters

The Jamestown settlers faced extreme difficulty from the outset,
and many men fell to disease, starved to death, or died in skirmishes with Native Americans. Only the adventurer **John
Smith**'s military expertise and leadership saved the colony. By
the time another English ship arrived in 1609, only fifty-three of
the original 100 colonists remained. Unfortunately, the ship carried 400 more settlers without any supplies. Overwhelmed and
suffering from battle injuries, Smith abandoned the colony and
returned to England.

The "Starving Time"

Smith's departure and the advent of winter marked the beginning of the **"starving time"** in Jamestown. Weak from disease and hunger, the 450 colonists destroyed the town for firewood and then barricaded themselves inside their fort to evade hostile natives. Once inside the fort, they resorted to eating dogs, rats, and even one another after food supplies disappeared. Only sixty people survived the winter. As the survivors prepared to abandon the colony the following spring, four English ships arrived with 500 more men and supplies. Settlers struggled for two more years until colonist **John Rolfe** discovered a new American treasure: tobacco.

Cash Crop: Tobacco

Rolfe discovered that the soil in and around Jamestown was perfectly suited for growing tobacco, and England and the rest of Europe couldn't buy enough of it. In fact, so many Europeans smoked or sniffed tobacco that Jamestown had exported thirty tons' worth of leaves to England by 1619. As a result, the little colony prospered and so did Virginia Company investors. At last, stockholders and the monarchy found it profitable to fund expeditions to the Americas. More important, the discovery of tobacco solidified England's position in North America.

To glean a share of the wealth, Parliament and the Crown forbade the colonists from shipping their tobacco anywhere but England. Even with the limited market, tobacco generated enough profit that the colonists grew richer too. Women eventually joined the farmers in Virginia as the colony flourished. Some Jamestown settlers also brought back black **indentured servants** (not slaves) who became the first Africans in North America.

Bacon's Rebellion

Historians have long looked on **Bacon's Rebellion** as the first manifestation of "revolutionary" feelings. In 1676, colonists in Virginia, especially on the western frontier of the colony, had come under attack from some of the Native American tribes in the area. The royal governor, Sir William Berkeley, had ordered an investigation into the attacks and arranged several meetings between the colonists and the Indians. **Nathaniel Bacon**, a farmer and landowner—and Berkeley's cousin—was unhappy with these efforts. He and several other farmers felt that the government was not protecting them. They coalesced into a loose army and began attacking largely peaceful Indian camps throughout northern Virginia.

Berkeley, in trying to keep the peace, labeled Bacon a rebel. Bacon and his forces surrounded the government buildings in Jamestown and forced Berkeley to flee the city. Shortly thereafter, Bacon died and Berkeley was able to return to power. He promptly hung several of Bacon's compatriots.

> *Bacon's Rebellion is the first instance historians point to of an independent spirit in the colonies. Bacon and his compatriots took matters into their own hands, and while the outcome was not what they had intended, the idea that they could change their lot in life by rising up against the government was one that had never before been visible in the colonies.*

THE PILGRIMS

The **Pilgrims**, who eventually established **Plymouth Colony**, belonged to an uncompromising sect of Protestant Puritans in England who challenged the Anglican Church's authority. Also known as **Separatists** because they had separated from the Anglican Church, these Pilgrims formed a Puritan church under their own covenant. Doing so was considered treasonous at the time, since the church and state were intertwined. To avoid imprisonment or persecution, the Pilgrims fled to Holland in 1607.

New World Freedom

Although the Dutch tolerated Puritan religious practices and allowed them to worship freely, the Pilgrim separatists found themselves relegated to performing the lowest-paying jobs. Living in poverty and finding that their children were assimilating into Dutch culture, the Pilgrim congregation made a drastic decision to leave Europe and establish a Puritan colony in the New World. Although the King of England didn't relish the idea of a faith-based settlement in North America, he agreed not to interfere.

The Mayflower Voyage

Securing a land patent from the Virginia Company, the Pilgrims created their own joint-stock company and prepared for the trans-Atlantic voyage. In 1620, 102 men, women, and children crowded aboard the *Mayflower* and set sail for America. Several non-Puritan settlers joined them, including a cooper named **John Alden** and a hired soldier named **Miles Standish**, both of whom played a crucial role in the founding of the colony. During the voyage, the Pilgrims were blown off course. Reaching Cape Cod instead of Virginia, they attempted to head south but had to turn back because of rough seas. The Pilgrims decided to stay on Cape Cod at a place they called Plymouth.

Assistance from Native Americans

The *Mayflower* remained in New England that first winter and provided shelter to the Pilgrims while they tried to build houses on land. Exposure to the elements, malnutrition, and illness soon began to take their toll, and more than half of the Pilgrims died that first winter. The settlers made friends with their neighbors, the Wampanoag Indians, who helped the remainder survive. One Wampanoag named **Squanto** helped the Pilgrims grow maize the next year. By the following autumn, the Pilgrims had their own bumper crop of corn and were well on their way to self-sufficiency.

To celebrate their bountiful first harvest, the Pilgrims held a feast and invited their Wampanoag neighbors. This feast served as the inspiration for the modern-day Thanksgiving holiday.

The Mayflower Compact

By the early seventeenth century, the king had divided English territorial claims in North America between two chartered joint-stock companies, the **London Virginia Company**, which had jurisdiction over the land from present-day North Carolina to New Jersey, and the **Plymouth Virginia Company**, which controlled the land from New York to Maine. Each company would then issue patents to groups of settlers, allowing them to establish settlements on company land.

The Pilgrims had settled what is now Massachusetts with their patent from the Virginia Company and were therefore outside the jurisdiction of either company. Since, technically, no one controlled them, the Pilgrims formed their own government under the **Mayflower Compact**. Forty-one men signed the compact, elected a simple government, and agreed to obey its laws.

MASSACHUSETTS BAY COLONY

Within a few years, a new colony of Puritans overshadowed the smaller Plymouth Colony. In 1629, a group of Puritan merchants and country gentlemen obtained a royal charter to found the **Massachusetts Bay Company**. The stockholders elected **John Winthrop**, a prosperous and respected lawyer and landowner, to serve as governor of the new colony. Unlike all previous charters from the king, the articles included the provision that the government of the Massachusetts Bay Colony could be located in the colony itself rather than in England. Winthrop and a group of 1,000 Puritans settled in Boston and Salem, Massachusetts, in 1630.

Reform vs. Separation

Winthrop's settlers were Puritans, but as they were not members of the Separatists' extreme sect, they were not Pilgrims, like the people of Plymouth. Instead, the Puritans in Boston and Salem believed that the Anglican Church just needed to be purified in order to restore strict biblical interpretations. In short, they were **Reformists**, not Separatists.

"City Upon a Hill"

Winthrop remained the leader of the Massachusetts Bay Colony for twenty years until his death in 1649. During this time, the colony grew rapidly, as nearly 20,000 Puritans fled England for the Salem and Boston area within the first ten years of the colony's existence. This contingent of Reformists planned to establish a shining example of Puritanism for the world and change the Anglican Church through the example of their good works and holy lifestyle.

Winthrop laid out this philosophy of setting an example for others to follow in a famous sermon. While still aboard the ship *Arbella* on the way from England, Winthrop delivered the sermon that has since been hailed one of the most famous and influential speeches in American history. Winthrop told the settlers they would be casting off all the evil and past wrongdoings of Europe and starting a new chapter in human history. He also proclaimed that the New World held the potential for greatness, saying, "We must consider that we shall be a city upon a hill. The eyes of all people are upon us." Winthrop's **"City Upon a Hill"** sermon thus pronounced the colony a beacon of godliness for the world.

This vision of America as "city upon a hill" for the entire world to see and emulate has been enormously influential in U.S. politics. Many political leaders and presidents have quoted Winthrop's speech at key points in their careers, including John Adams, Abraham Lincoln, John F. Kennedy, Ronald Reagan, and Bill Clinton, among many others.

Halfway Covenant

The foundation of the Puritans in the New World was shortly thereafter marked by an important change in the church: how membership was conferred. Up until 1677, membership in the Puritan church was restricted to those who could give verbal testimony of their "experience of Grace." Even those baptized had to pass this testimony before being accepted as full members of the church. In 1622, however, came the publication of the **Halfway Covenants**, adopted to allow certain people to retain a limited degree of church privileges, including baptizing their children, without becoming offical members. In 1677, this new practice was adopted and greatly increased the sizes of congregations in the New World.

THE MIDDLE COLONIES

In the seventeenth century, mostly all the colonists believed the church instilled moral behavior and respect for authority and created better citizens. The governments relied on the church and protected its existence in a reciprocal relationship. As a result, each of the early English colonies established its own state-sanctioned church. All the early colonial leaders in the southern Virginian colonies and the northern Puritan colonies believed everyone in the colony should practice the same religion to maintain unity. They also reasoned there would be no religious persecution if there was only one faith to follow. In other words, each colony would be harmonious without any religious or civic disagreements.

The middle colonies, comprising New York, New Jersey, Pennsylvania, and Delaware, however, did not establish state-sanctioned religions. In refusing to do so, they opened the doors to people from a **multitude of nationalities and faiths**.

The mid-Atlantic region, unlike New England or the southern colonies, drew many of its initial settlers from war-torn or intolerant countries in Europe. Those who fled to the middle colonies of the New World included:

- Dutch Mennonites

- French Huguenots

- German Baptists

- Portuguese Jews

- Dutch Reformed

- Lutherans

- Quakers

All of these groups had borne the brunt of religious exclusion in Europe and were not eager to repeat the experience in the New World. They joined Anglicans already living in the middle colonies and simply agreed to disagree. Add to the mix the indigenous people and the African slaves (with their own religious practices), and the middle colonies become a mosaic of nationalities and religious practices.

New York. Originally called New Netherlands, the English renamed the colony New York after defeating the former Dutch owners in 1664. New York City eventually became a port of entry and home for people of all nationalities. In a census taken in 1770, for example, there were eighteen different churches to support a population of 22,000 people: three Dutch Reformed, three Anglican, three Presbyterian, two Lutheran, one French Huguenot, one Congregational, one Methodist, one Baptist, one Quaker, one Moravian, and one Jewish temple.

New Jersey. The colony of New Jersey developed more slowly than New York, but its diversity was just as great. By 1701, the colony had forty-five different congregations. Most were unable to afford individual churches, so they frequently shared houses of worship.

Pennsylvania. William Penn formed the colony of Pennsylvania to provide a safe haven for the persecuted through the old and new worlds. Although a Quaker himself, Penn believed that force would never convert anyone. Many persecuted peoples such as the Amish, Dunkers, Schwenkfelders, and Mennonites found freedom in Pennsylvania.

Delaware. Scandinavian Lutherans and Dutch Reformed were the first to settle Delaware, and English Quakers and Welsh Baptists soon followed. Although Delaware was one of the most diverse colonies, the Anglican Church had a strong following there by the end of the eighteenth century.

Cast out of Puritan Salem and Plymouth for his radical beliefs, **Roger Williams** *founded the colony of Providence, Rhode Island, in 1636. Providence was the first permanent settlement in Rhode Island and one of the first along with Pennsylvania to legislate freedom of religion.*

Discuss how the Halfway Covenant and Bacon's Rebellion reflected the social and political tensions in early colonial America.

The motivation for English colonization revolved around religious and economic incentives. By the end of the seventeenth century, two distinctive English colonies had emerged in America. The Puritans established the Massachusetts Bay Colony in pursuit of religious purity and John Winthrop's vision of a "City Upon a Hill." Alternatively, Virginia was chartered as a joint-stock company, which attracted entrepreneurs willing to venture stakes in tobacco. During the colonial period, both regions experienced hardships that slowly pulled each colony away from its founding principles. The Halfway Covenant and Bacon's Rebellion not only reflected the underlying social and political tensions but also helped to create a new understanding of community.

The Halfway Covenant was an indirect concession that the Puritan way of life was in jeopardy. Second- and third-generation Puritans had strayed from the strict ways of the founders and were looking for an easing of church standards. As originally conceived, the elect Puritans were the only ones entitled to the rite of Baptism. In order to become a "saint," an individual had to endure the process of public conversion. This process involved an intense scrutiny of one's life and offered no guarantees for selection. Facing the unsettling prospect of unbaptized grandchildren, the original saints were willing to compromise. The publication and adoption of Halfway Covenant enabled the children of saints to be baptized but denied them the privileges of Communion and voting in church affairs. Increasing numbers of Puritans accepted "halfway" status, which eventually left the saints in the minority. The Halfway Covenant responded to the demands of contemporary Puritans and signaled an erosion of the community's founding principles. In the process, the Puritans moved toward a more inclusive and secular society.

The tension in New England was not isolated and could also be seen in the growing discontent in the Chesapeake Bay region.

Student Essay

Bacon's Rebellion in Virginia was the pinnacle of this unrest. From the colony's inception, Virginia's prosperity was dependent on tobacco farming. The profits yielded from tobacco led to a polarized division of wealth. A powerful merchant class relied upon a large work force, which was initially supplied by indentured servants. The division continued to widen as indentured servants who had fulfilled their servitude were forced to move farther inland (since the most profitable land was already owned by the wealthy). The new land was less productive and forced more interaction with the Indians. After years of tension along the frontier, a series of attacks against the colonists sparked Bacon's Rebellion. Bacon organized a few hundred men who were frustrated by financial strains—especially after the Tobacco Depression—and the governor's costly proposal to establish a line of forts along the frontier. After a couple of successful raids, Bacon looked to wage an all-out war on the Indians, and his support swelled to over a thousand men. The governor was forced to give his support to Bacon, but he soon renounced it. Angered at being called back, Bacon set off for Jamestown, and his men proceeded to burn it to the ground. The rebellion came to a quick end after Bacon fell ill and died. Although his supporters went their separate ways, their frustration actually fostered a new sense of community. The previous division of class dissolved as colonists banded together along racial lines.

The conflicts of the colonial period have a pivotal place in early American history. The set of circumstances that resulted in the Halfway Covenant and Bacon's Rebellion was unique to each region but helped forge common social grounds. The relaxing of Puritan strictness and the increased appreciation of community in Virginia enabled the colonists to begin the unifying process. The social and political tension and the desire to relieve it would continue to move America on its course toward revolution.

Test Questions and Answers

1. *How might the terms "Age of Exploration" and "Age of Exploitation" describe the same period in different ways?*

   - The term *exploration* denotes all the positive outcomes of Europeans exploring the New World, including the opening of new markets and the discovery of new resources.

   - The term *exploitation* denotes all the negative ramifications of European contact with the New World, such as the destruction of Native American lives via disease and warfare.

2. *What was European society like on the eve of Columbus's discovery of the New World?*

   - Technological advances like gunpowder and navigational instruments were making it possible for Europe to explore the world.

   - The Renaissance, a revival of learning, was opening people's minds to new possibilities and ideas.

   - Towns and cities were growing and becoming important centers of trade.

   - A capitalist economy was emerging with stockholders, new corporations, and a merchant class facilitating business growth.

   - New nation-states were emerging with powerful monarchies holding enough territory and wealth to sponsor exploration.

3. *Trace the development and impact of Spanish settlement in the Americas.*

   - The Spanish claimed that their motives for exploration were to spread Christianity and to gain material wealth.

   - Conquistadores initially conquered much of Mexico, Central, and South America before moving into the southwestern portion of what is now the United States.

- Spanish exploration had an enormous impact on the local indigenous peoples: many of the natives died from disease or from being forced into slavery.

- When Native Americans proved to be poor slave laborers, the Spanish imported African slaves and thus began the mass movement of millions of Africans to the Americas.

4. Why did the British find colonization in North America so difficult?

- Most colonies suffered under poor leadership.

- Settlers had difficulty getting along with the local Native Americans.

- Disease and rugged terrain plagued settlers in the southern colonies around Virginia.

Timeline

c. 800–900	Vikings colonize Iceland, Greenland, and Newfoundland.
c. 1300–1600	Europe experiences the Renaissance.
1325	The Aztecs found Tenochtitlán (later known as Mexico City).
1440	Johann Gutenberg invents the moveable-type press.
1492	Christopher Columbus lands on an island in the West Indies and names it San Salvador.
1493	Columbus returns to the Americas on his second voyage.
1521	Hernando Cortés conquers the Aztecs.
1532	Pizarro defeats the Incas.
1539–1542	Spanish explorer Hernando De Soto and 600 soldiers trek through what later becomes the southern United States.
1587	Sir Walter Raleigh founds Roanoke, off the coast of North Carolina.
1588	England defeats the Spanish Armada.
1607	The Virginia Company founds Jamestown.
1609–1610	Colonists in Jamestown suffer the "starving time," an extremely harsh winter.
1612	Colonist John Rolfe begins growing tobacco in Virginia.
1620	Pilgrims sail to America on the *Mayflower* and found the colony of Plymouth in Massachussetts. They also sign the Mayflower Compact, establishing their own government.
1629	The Massachusetts Bay Colony obtains a royal charter and elects John Winthrop as governor.
	Winthrop gives his "City Upon a Hill" sermon.
1636	Roger Williams founds Providence in Rhode Island, the first settlement to legislate freedom of religion.
1662	Halfway Covenant enacted.
1664	English settlers conquer the Dutch settlement of New Netherlands and rename it New York.
1676	Bacon's Rebellion occurs.

Major Figures

John Alden   Although not a Puritan himself, John Alden sailed across the Atlantic on the *Mayflower* with the Pilgrims and helped found and lead Plymouth Colony.

Nathaniel Bacon   A farmer and landowner, Bacon formed a loose army and rose up against Native American camps in Virginia. Later known as Bacon's Rebellion, this was the first sign of colonial rebelling.

Jacques Cartier   A French explorer, Cartier made three early voyages into present-day Canada in the early 1500s.

Samuel de Champlain   A French explorer, Champlain founded "New France," present-day eastern Canada, in the 1600s.

Hernando Cortés   A Spanish *conquistador*, Cortés conquered the Aztecs and took their capital of Tenochititlán (Mexico City) in 1521.

Christopher Columbus   An Italian explorer, Columbus discovered the New World in 1492 when he lands on an island in the Caribbean.

Hernando De Soto   A Spanish explorer and *conquistador*, De Soto trekked through the present-day southwestern portion of the United States for Spain in the mid-1500s.

Francisco Pizarro   A Spanish explorer and conquistador, Pizarro conquered the Inca Empire in the 1520s and claimed all the land from Panama to Peru for Spain.

Sir Walter Raleigh   Half-brother of Sir Humphrey Gilbert, Raleigh obtained a royal charter in 1587 to found the colony of Roanoke in Virginia. The colonists, however, mysteriously disappeared between the time of settlement and 1590.

John Rolfe   A colonist of Jamestown, Rolfe saved the colony in Virginia when he discovered tobacco. His discovery also gave England further cause to establish more colonies in North America. Rolfe also promoted peaceful relations with the Indians by marrying Pocahontas.

John Smith A mercenary, Smith took command of the Jamestown colony in the early 1600s and thus saved the colonists from starvation and hostile Native Americans.

Squanto A member of the Wampanoag tribe of present-day Massachusetts, Squanto helped the Pilgrims at Plymouth learn how to survive in the harsh New England environment.

Miles Standish A soldier hired by the Puritans who sailed to North America on the *Mayflower*, Standish proved instrumental to the early success of Plymouth Plantation.

Amerigo Vespucci An Italian explorer, Vespucci published a wildly popular account of his voyages in the New World near the North American continent in 1503. A German mapmaker named the new continents after him to honor his achievements.

Roger Williams A cast-out from Puritan Salem and Plymouth because of his radical religious beliefs, Williams founded his own colony of Providence, which became the first permanent settlement in Rhode Island.

John Winthrop A prosperous and respected lawyer and landowner, Winthrop served as the governor of the Massachusetts Bay Colony. He claimed that Americans stood distinct from Europeans and had an opportunity to usher in a new age for humanity in his famous "City Upon the Hill" speech.

Suggested Reading

• Bradford, William. *Of Plymouth Plantation 1620–1647*. New York: Vision Forum, 1999.

This is Bradford's personal journal about the lives of the Puritans at Plymouth. One of the few firsthand accounts of life in Plymouth, it is an excellent telling of what the Pilgrims faced in the New World.

• Pagden, Anthony. *European Encounters with the New World: From Renaissance to Romanticism*. New Haven, Connecticut: Yale University Press, 1994.

Pagden examines the impact of the discovery and exploration of the New World on Old World Europe and how the Native Americans in turn perceived these explorers. Much is devoted to how these perceptions led to the hostilities between these two cultures throughout the colonial period.

• Todorov, Tzvetan. *The Conquest of America: The Question of the Other*. Norman: University of Oklahoma Press, 1992.

This 1992 book reexamines the nature of the Spanish conquest of America, taking a sociological approach to understanding how both the Spanish and the Native Americans must have interpreted the prescence and actions of each other.

Colonial Life: 1700–1763

- Southern Colonies
- Northern Colonies
- Colonial Cities
- Slavery
- The Enlightenment
- The Great Awakening
- British Rule
- The French and Indian War

There were greater opportunities in America than the colonists could have ever hoped for in Europe. Yet as a distinctive "American" identity was being formed, the colonists still held on to many traditions and characteristics of the Old World. Social stratifications, for example, still existed, though to a lesser extent than in Europe. At the same time, there was more potential for social mobility as many Americans had opportunities to change jobs and their position in life.

Although the thirteen English colonies had much in common, factors such as geography and climate soon created distinct differences. These differences would become more and more pronounced as the colonies swelled in size, and, many years later, would eventually threaten to tear the country apart in ways the colonists in 1700 could never imagine.

Southern Colonies

The southern colonies included Maryland, Virginia, North Carolina, South Carolina, and Georgia. These colonies all boasted plenty of good, cleared land and a mild climate conducive to growing staple and exotic cash crops. Tobacco became the staple crop and the economic foundation of Virginia and North Carolina. South Carolinian soil, though unfit for tobacco, was perfect for growing rice and indigo, a dye used to dye textiles blue. The southern colonies also produced lumber, tar, pitch, turpentine, furs, and cattle.

> In colonial times, blue paint was a status symbol, as the dye was expensive and hard to come by. Many well-to-do colonists desired to have their houses painted blue.

WORK IN THE SOUTHERN COLONIES

The production of cash crops required large amounts of land and a large work force. Colonists had plenty of land, but not enough labor. **Indentured servants** performed much of the labor during the early years of colonization. These servants, mostly paupers from England, Ireland, and Germany, got their name from the indenture, or contract, they signed, binding themselves to work for a period of four to seven years to pay for their transportation to the New World. Many of northern Europe's poor voluntarily indentured themselves in order to acquire their own land after their contract had been fulfilled. Indentured servants accounted for roughly half of all white settlers living in the colonies outside New England.

Until the latter half of the 1600s, white indentured servants were the dominant source of labor in the Americas, and it was not until the 1680s and 1690s that slave labor began to surpass the use of white indentured servants. Although **African slaves** cost more initially than indentured servants, they served for life and thus quickly became the labor force of choice on large plantations.

LIFE IN THE EARLY COLONIAL SOUTH

In the early 1600s, most southern colonists lived in utter poverty, and men outnumbered women three to one. Southern colonists suffered high mortality rates because of the many mosquito-born illnesses that plagued the land. As a result, the average southern man could expect to live only forty years, while southern women usually did not live past their late thirties. Moreover, one-quarter of all children born in the southern colonies died in infancy, and half died before they reached adulthood. Most southern colonists lived in remote areas on farms or plantations with their families, extended relatives, friends, and slaves. The Anglican religion dominated the region, although most southerners did not attend church regularly, if at all.

By the 1700s, life had settled down for the southern colonists, and more rigid social classes had formed. A gentry, or wealthy upper class, emerged and built large plantation homes in an attempt to imitate the lives of the English upper crust. Many of the plantation owners relied heavily on credit to maintain their leisurely lifestyles.

Northern Colonies

The northern colonies included New Hampshire, Massachusetts, Rhode Island, Connecticut, New York, and New Jersey. Whereas southerners lived in relative isolation from one another, northern colonial life revolved around townships. Villages formed around the church, and a central green area was usually created (often called "the commons") where important business and community activities took place. People built their houses around the town center and then radiated out in concentric circles. As a result, community involvement and activity became a central feature of life in the North.

States and Territories before the Louisiana Purchase

WORK IN THE NORTHERN COLONIES

Most of the land in the North was stony, sloped, and heavily for-ested, and people in the North couldn't sustain huge plantations as their southern neighbors could. Instead, families farmed small plots with the help of perhaps one or two servants or slaves. Addi-tionally, the weather was too cold and harsh to support large-scale market crops. As a result, northern farmers mainly grew crops for their own consumption and sold any surplus at local markets. Crops like barley, oats, and wheat were mainly grown; the colonists also raised cattle, pigs, and sheep. Many northern-ers became fishermen. Skilled artisans migrated to the northern colonies, developing industries that ultimately created a founda-tion for future manufacturing.

Ample water sources made the construction of mills possible to process grain, textiles, and lumber. In time, a strong merchant class emerged, bolstered by the shipping industry that developed in northern ports. As shipping grew, ship building also increased. Eventually, traders and bankers sprang up to run the manufacturing and shipping economy, and northern port cities like Boston became central trading areas for the British in the Americas.

LIFE IN THE EARLY COLONIAL NORTH

The northern climate was free of mosquitoes, so northerners enjoyed longer lives, usually living well into their sixties, as compared with their southern counterparts. Husbands and wives formed teams of production, with children adding to the number of workers. The single life was almost impossible, given both the religious climate and the physical rigors of life in general at the time.

In contrast to the southern colonies, religion permeated the lives of northern colonists and exercised a pervasive influence over the people. Towns and communities were built around the church, and in most colonies, the church and the state remained one, controlling many aspects of life. Puritans settled in New England, both separatists and reformists, and these rigid religions dominated the region.

The Salem Witch Trials

Increasing influences from the outside world, introduced by new immigrants, among other sources, strained northern society, as the tragedy of the 1692 **Salem witch trials** made clear. Salem had been settled by Puritan reformists, and like most people in the North at this time, they still believed in the supernatural. By 1691, nearly 300 primarily middle-aged women in New England had been convicted of witchcraft. Of those, more than thirty were hanged.

The episode in Salem was far more intense than any other witch-hunt in North America. It began during the winter of 1691–1692, when several adolescent girls accused three local women of practicing witchcraft. Similar accusations followed, and within a year, nineteen women had been hanged, one man pressed to death under heavy stones, and more than 100 others jailed.

New Roles for Women

Historians originally thought that local feuds and property disputes between the town of Salem proper and Salem Village caused the unrest. More recently, many historians have begun to believe that the trials resulted from the clash between two different sets of social values. Many of the accused women had in some way defied the traditional roles assigned to females. Some worked outside the home, while others did not attend church. Whatever the reason, no other similar outbreaks of mass hysteria occurred in New England.

Colonial Cities

The thirteen British colonies developed separately and distinctly throughout the seventeenth century. In fact, the large cities of Boston, New York, Philadelphia, and Charleston had more contact with London than they did with one another. Traveling between cities on crude roads was both difficult and dangerous, which contributed to the isolation. However, taverns provided safe havens, overnight rest stops, and refueling stations. Colonists gathered in taverns to relax, drink, and gossip about politics and business. Many years later, these tendencies would prove vital to both the exchange of information about British injustices and to promoting the efforts of the revolution.

Despite the fact that 90 percent of all colonists lived in townships and small villages in the countryside, the minority of city dwellers controlled commerce, dominated politics, and defined the cultural norms. Society was rigidly stratified in cities, with merchants at the top of the order; craftsmen, retailers, and innkeepers below them; and sailors, unskilled workers, and small artisans at the bottom. Over time, class stratification became more pronounced, and wealth became concentrated among a select few. All of the colonists, however, hungered for English luxury goods. Imports increased through the years as the Americans purchased more and more goods such as mirrors, silver-plated items, spices, linens, wigs, clocks, tea sets, books, and other household items.

Slavery

Slavery had virtually disappeared in Western Europe by the 1500s, and only Spain and Portugal still practiced slavery. Unfortunately, they brought slavery with them to the New World, where it established a strong foothold.

THE FIRST SLAVE TRADERS

The Portuguese were the first Europeans to trade with Africa and the first to reap the enormous profits to be made in the slave trade. By the time Columbus sailed for the Americas, the Portuguese had taken about 25,000 Africans to work on sugar plantations. The Spanish recognized the labor potential of slaves and began importing them to the New World to mine for gold and silver.

THE MIDDLE PASSAGE

Other European countries also became involved in the slave trade. In addition to the Spanish and Portuguese, the English, French, and Dutch actively bought and sold Africans into slavery. These Europeans used extreme violence and brutal tactics to acquire their slaves.

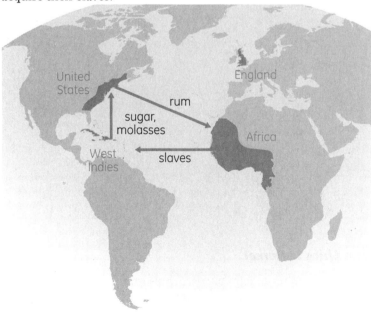

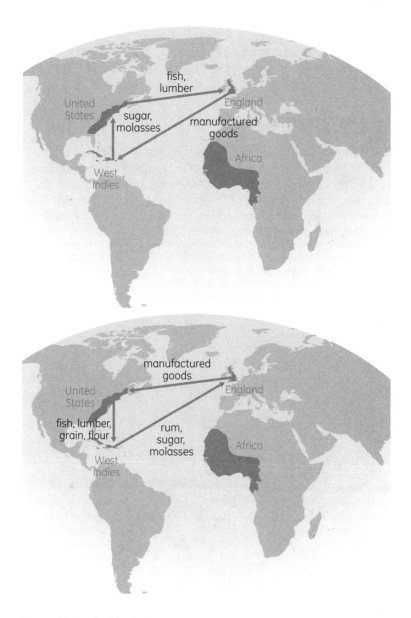

From Africa to Market

Slaves suffered unimaginable hardships on the Middle Passage. Slave traders often packed as many Africans aboard their ships as

*The Triangular Trade The trans-Atlantic voyage from Africa to the Americas was known as the Middle Passage and was part of a larger shipping pattern known as the **Triangular Trade**, linking Africa, the Americas, and Europe. Slaves traveled from Africa to the Americas; sugar and raw materials would be shipped to Europe; tobacco, timber, and foodstuffs would be shipped from North America to the West Indies.*

possible in order to maximize profits. In addition to depression, slaves suffered from smallpox, measles, gonorrhea, syphilis, yellow fever, scurvy, and dysentery. On average, about 12.5 percent of the captive slaves died during the voyage.

Once they had arrived in the New World, slaves had to endure the **"seasoning"** process, or the period ranging from a few months to a year in which slavers prepared them for sale and life as a slave. Historians estimate that 30 percent of imported Africans died of disease or maltreatment during "seasoning."

Growth of Slavery in the Americas

Between 1492 and 1808, slave traders brought roughly 10 million Africans to the New World, mostly to Spanish or Portuguese plantations in South America and the West Indies. Even though only 400,000 of these slaves traveled to North America, all thirteen colonies had legalized slavery by 1750. Many colonial farmers came to prefer slavery as rising wages in England made it more and more difficult to find indentured servants.

In time, slavery became more acceptable and developed into a key aspect of the economy and American society. States developed laws to keep African Americans under control: whipping, branding, dismembering, castrating, or killing a slave became legal under certain circumstances. Laws also stripped slaves of the freedom of movement, freedom of assembly, and the right to earn money or pursue an education. White Americans feared a slave rebellion above all else, especially considering that slaves outnumbered whites in some areas. Slave revolts in Charleston, South Carolina (1739) and New York City (1741) fueled these fears.

The Enlightenment

During the flurry of exploration and colonization in North America in the seventeenth and eighteenth centuries, Europe was experiencing a scientific revolution known as the **Enlightenment**. Scientists had abandoned the old Ptolemaic view of an earth-centered universe in favor of Copernicus's heliocentric (sun-centered) model. Isaac Newton had published his theory of gravitation, which laid the foundation for a scientific vision of the universe and argued that events occur in accordance with natural laws. More important, people were using reason and the study of mathematics to understand the working of the universe and the world around them.

Philosophers of the Enlightenment like John Locke believed that the American experience embodied the ideas of the Enlightenment. The old barriers of birth and wealth did not apply as much in the New World as they did in Europe, and people of all classes could succeed if they worked hard.

JOHN LOCKE'S CONTRACT THEORY OF GOVERNMENT

John Locke applied the new scientific understandings of the world first presented in the Enlightenment to the study of society and government. Locke came up with an idea he called the **Theory of Contract under Natural Law**, in which he argued that kings and queens did not hold their positions because of God's divine will but because of an accident of birth. In other words, kings had simply gotten lucky. Locke further explained that all humans had certain natural rights such as the rights to life, liberty, and property, and that no government could deny its constituents these rights.

Locke's theory on government had an enormous influence on American political thought. Locke argued that the people "contracted" with the government to protect their interests. If the government failed to do so, then the government had broken the contract and should be disbanded. Colonists quickly picked up on this idea, eventually using it to justify the American Revolution against England. In fact, Thomas Jefferson used very similar language in the Declaration of Independence when he wrote that everyone had the right to "life, liberty, and the pursuit of happiness."

BENJAMIN FRANKLIN

Benjamin Franklin, one of the "founding fathers" of the country, personified the ideas of the Enlightenment. Franklin owned his own print shop, published his own newspaper, and had published his *Poor Richard's Almanac* all by the time he had turned twenty-six. Franklin's business was so successful that he retired when he was only forty-two, and he devoted the rest of his life to science and public service. Among other things, Franklin:

- Founded a library and invented a new kind of stove

- Started an academy that eventually became the University of Pennsylvania

- Formed a debating club that eventually became the American Philosophical Society

- Wrote a treatise entitled *Experiments and Observations on Electricity*, based on his own electrical experiments

- Studied medicine, meteorology, geology, astronomy, and physics

- Served his country as the colonial agent in London and then as the American ambassador to France during the Revolutionary War

Franklin was a living example of Locke's ideas of the possibilities that society and government had to offer.

The Great Awakening

With so many new scientific and philosophical ideas springing out of the Enlightenment, many American colonists turned away from religion. In the 1730s, however, a renewed spirit of evangelism swept through the colonies in the **Great Awakening**. In an attempt to reassert the doctrines of Puritanism, the leading preachers and theologians of the Great Awakening appealed very strongly to colonists' emotions.

GEORGE WHITEFIELD

The Great Awakening began in different cities in the colonies, but all the revivals shared a high level of emotionalism. Preachers such as **George Whitefield** tried to replace the cold and unfeeling doctrines of Puritanism with a religion more accessible to the average person. The twenty-seven-year-old Wesleyan minister noted upon arriving in the colonies from England that American congregations lacked passion because "dead men preach to them."

Planning to reignite the fires of religion in the New World, Whitefield settled in Philadelphia in 1739 and began attracting crowds of more than 6,000 people. Before long, he was holding revivals from as far south as Georgia all the way up to New England. Young and charismatic, Whitefield staged performances for his audiences by acting out the miseries of hell and the joys of salvation. People flocked from miles around to hear him speak, and he urged them to experience a "new birth," or a sudden, emotional moment of conversion and forgiveness of sin. Audiences swooned with anticipation of God's grace, some people writhing, some laughing out loud, and some crying out for help.

JONATHAN EDWARDS

Jonathan Edwards was another noteworthy preacher and theologian during the Great Awakening. He believed that his parishioners, especially the young, lived too freely, spending their time drinking and carousing while the older churchgoers had become preoccupied with making and spending money. Edwards wanted to touch the hearts of those in his congregation and "fright persons away from hell." He would therefore fill his sermons with vivid descriptions of the torments of hell and the pleasures of heaven. By 1735, he reported that "the town seemed to be full of the presence of God; it never was so full of love, nor of joy."

Unlike Whitefield, Edwards never resorted to theatrics, and instead entranced audiences with the seriousness of his message, as in his most famous sermon **"Sinners in the Hands of an Angry God,"** which marked the pinnacle of the Great Awakening movement and is recognized as one of the most famous sermons in American history.

IMPACT OF THE GREAT AWAKENING

The Great Awakening had an enormous impact in the American colonies, especially along the western frontier and in the South. Common folk responded with great enthusiasm, and the Baptists and the Methodists, two popular Protestant denominations, grew enormously as a result.

Ironically, even though revivalists like Whitefield and Edwards had hoped they would encourage a more pious lifestyle, the colonists concluded that salvation was available to all, not merely to a few chosen elect as the Puritans had always claimed. Consequently, the Great Awakening helped democratize religion in the colonies and ultimately took power away from churches and ministers. Moreover, the Great Awakening renewed interest in intellectualism and prompted the founding of new universities and the distribution of books.

> *Some historians argue that the American Revolution could not have happened without the Great Awakening. They believe that the Awakening encouraged spiritual diversity and emphasized the personal dimensions of salvation, undermining the dogmatic religious institutions of the day. In turn, this spiritual diversity paved the way for the eventual separation of church and state, which became a crucial component of the American conception of freedom.*

CHAPTER 2
1700–1763

British Rule

By the 1750s, the American colonists, feeling more unified by such intellectual currents as the Enlightenment and the Great Awakening, had developed a unique culture of their own. Although the individual colonies developed distinctive religious, social, and demographic characteristics, they all shared a basic sense of unity that grew stronger through the coming years of economic and political upheaval.

The colonists had effectively governed themselves throughout most of the seventeenth and eighteenth centuries. For the most part, the British government had left the colonists to fend for themselves during this **Age of Salutary Neglect,** neither imposing new taxes nor enforcing those on the books. Therefore, the colonists resented Britain's attempts to exert more influence over the colonies in the mid-1700s.

BRITISH TRADE WITH THE COLONIES

Although the British had granted the colonies a fair amount of autonomy, they had always attempted to control trade to and from North America. The British imposed laws and taxes to ensure that all trade with the colonies would benefit Britain, and to ensure that the colonists did not take trade matters into their own hands.

The Mercantile System

Under the **Mercantile System**, power and wealth went hand in hand. In other words, the leaders of mercantilist countries (countries with large import and export operations) believed that power derived from a full national treasury. To acquire and keep gold and silver, the mercantilist powers had to limit foreign imports and preserve a favorable balance of trade. To do this, England, France, Spain, Portugal, and the Netherlands:

- Encouraged their domestic manufacturers to produce as many goods as possible

- Developed and protected their own shipping industry

- Acquired colonies to provide raw materials

- Sold finished manufactured goods to the colonists

Under mercantilism, great powers needed to acquire colonies to produce raw materials such as grain, sugar, rice, timber, and tobacco. Each colony also provided the mother country with an exclusive market for its manufactured goods. To safeguard its monopoly in North America, Britain began regulating colonial trade in the 1660s and declared that Americans could only ship their products directly to England. Royal officials could then levy taxes on those goods before shippers sent them elsewhere.

Navigation Acts

The **Navigation Act of 1660** marked England's first real attempt to regulate colonial trade by stipulating that all goods exported from the colonies had to be carried on English ships. The act also declared that colonists could only trade certain raw materials such as sugar, cotton, tobacco, wood, pitch, and tar with England or other British colonies. The **Second Navigation Act of 1663** required that colonial ships unload their cargo upon arriving in England so that each item could be taxed.

Restraining Acts

The **Restraining Acts of 1699** followed the Navigation Acts and protected manufacturers in England by banning factories in the colonies. Although colonial industry hadn't even begun to develop by this point, Britain didn't want colonial manufacturers to compete with domestic manufacturers in England. The Restraining Act also banned the export of woolen products in order to protect the English wool industry and later forbade the export of beaver hats and processed iron.

The Colonists' Response

Most colonists willingly complied with the Navigation and Restraining Acts, simply happy they had achieved a relatively high standard of living in such a short amount of time. More important, the restrictions on manufacturing affected few Americans because manufacturing hadn't ever taken root.

Moreover, the mercantile system showered the colonists with benefits. Even though the British levied taxes on American raw materials, they also kept prices on those materials high by eliminating foreign competition. Britain even paid subsidies to American shipbuilders and tobacco and rice farmers. In short, both sides benefited handsomely from the arrangement.

The Molasses Act

Despite economic benefits, some colonists had begun to complain about their subservient position within the mercantile system by the 1730s. The Navigation and Restraining Acts hit those who conducted trade in the West Indies hardest. In 1733, Britain passed the **Molasses Act** to curtail colonial trade with the West Indies by imposing a huge tax on sugar and molasses imported into the colonies. The act would have seriously disrupted colonial trade, but the royal officials in North America never strictly enforced it. This wavering policy led many Americans to question Britain's intentions and wisdom regarding the regulation of colonial trade.

COLONIAL GOVERNMENTS

King George III owned all the colonies, but Americans enjoyed an unprecedented degree of autonomy. All but one of the colonies had erected their own government with a bicameral legislature comprising an upper and lower house. The king appointed a governor and the members of the upper house in eight of the thirteen colonies. Wealthy land-owning colonists chose the members of the lower house. The colonies of Pennsylvania, Delaware, and Maryland were owned by individuals. These individuals, such as William Penn in Pennsylvania, held the royal charter and appointed legislators. In the corporate colonies of Rhode Island and Connecticut, owned by joint stock companies, wealthy land-owning white men elected all government officials.

Voting and Representation

Colonial governments modeled themselves after the English system with two exceptions:

- A greater percentage of the population could vote in the colonies than in England.

- The colonists rejected the British concept of **"virtual representation."** In England, elected members of Parliament claimed to represent all their constituents because they supposedly represented the interests of all royal subjects no matter where they lived. The colonists disagreed; they felt that delegates should represent only those who had elected them.

All in all, the representative colonial legislatures enjoyed a great deal of freedom, and the king permitted the autonomy as long as colonial laws didn't interfere with Parliament's.

The French and Indian War

For most of the colonial period, Britain and France remained at peace with each other, their colonial empires developing in relative isolation. Beginning in the 1680s, however, the European powers waged several wars for control of North America:

- The War of the Palatinate (King William's War) from 1689–1697 in New England and Canada

- The War of the Spanish Succession (Queen Anne's War) from 1702–1713 throughout the western frontier of the colonies from St. Augustine in Florida to New England

- The War of the Austrian Succession (King George's War) from 1744–1748 in Canada

- The Seven Years' War (the French and Indian War, which actually lasted nine years in the colonies) from 1754–1763 throughout New England and Canada

The British and the American colonists fought side by side against the French in all four wars, gaining much western land and parts of Canada as a result.

> The colonists referred to the Seven Years' War as the French and Indian War because they fought the French and Indians. The British called the war the Seven Years' War, because they didn't count the first two years that the war was fought only in the colonies.

THE FRENCH IN AMERICA

The French established their presence in the New World in the 1670s. Their mercantilist empire spanned from India to Africa to the Americas. The French king expected his North American settlers to export furs and grains back to France and then purchase French manufactured goods. By 1682, the French had sailed from Canada down the Mississippi, claiming land on both sides of the river, and founding the city of New Orleans.

By 1743, the French had reached the Rocky Mountains and claimed the entire interior of North America for themselves. To consolidate their claim, they built a string of forts that ran from Quebec to Detroit and down to New Orleans. The British, however, refused to recognize French territorial claims or the legality of the forts.

Indian Alliances

Both the British and the French knew that they would need the help of the local Native Americans with the skirmishes in the Americas. The British had established effective trading practices with the native tribes, but the French promised them friendship and equality and demonstrated a greater sensitivity to the Native Americans' cultures. French fur trappers, for example, frequently married Indian women and adopted native customs, while the Jesuit priests refrained from using force when trying to convert them to Catholicism.

THE WAR BEGINS

The **French and Indian War** began in 1754 when the governor of Virginia sent a young lieutenant colonel in the Virginia militia named **George Washington** to warn the French that the disputed Ohio Valley territory had been settled at France's peril. Washington carried the message to a French fort but was rebuffed. Soon afterward, he organized a force of volunteers, defeated a small French garrison, and built a modest outpost he called Fort Necessity. The French returned in greater numbers and attacked the fort, eventually forcing Washington to surrender and withdraw to Virginia. Washington's surrender triggered a series of Indian raids along the frontier, in which the Native Americans sought revenge for 150 years of bad treatment by the British.

The Fighting

Fighting raged for two years between the British and the French in the colonies before the war erupted in Europe. In 1756, the colonial war finally spilled over into Europe, when Austria and Russia and eventually Spain formed an alliance with France. Britain allied with Prussia in return. King George II named William Pitt the head of the war ministry, and Pitt tried to keep the focus of the war in North America. He sent large numbers of British troops to the colonies but also encouraged the colonists to enlist, demanding that they defend themselves against the French. Pitt's tactics worked, and the British eventually gained the upper hand. France simply couldn't match Britain's powerful navy or the number of troops stationed in North America.

The French and Indian War climaxed in 1759 when the British defeated the French at Quebec and effectively eliminated France's influence in North America. News of the battle reached London along with news of a similar victory in India, in which British forces had significantly reduced the number of French outposts. Outgunned and outnumbered, France formally surrendered in the Americas in September 1760. It took three more years before Britain could declare victory in Europe.

THE WAR ENDS

The **Treaty of Paris**, or Peace of Paris, ended the French and Indian War and gave Britain undisputed control over all of Canada and almost all of present-day United States, from the Atlantic to the Rockies. Britain decided to keep everything east of the Mississippi and gave Spain everything west of the Mississippi, including the key port city of New Orleans in exchange for Florida. Britain also gained control of several former French colonies in the Caribbean. In short, Britain reigned supreme over North America east of the Mississippi after the conclusion of the war.

IMPACT ON THE COLONIES

The French and Indian War had a tremendous impact on the colonists and on England. Britain's debt skyrocketed because it had had to borrow so much to fund the war, and Parliament decided to raise colonial taxes to pay off that debt. At the same time, Pitt's insistence that the colonists defend themselves added to the colonists' sense of independence from England. Success on the battlefield contributed to the colonists' belief that their reliance on England was coming to an end. Ultimately, the war boosted the new Americans' sense of unity and distinctiveness from Britain.

> At the beginning of the French and Indian War, Benjamin Franklin proposed a plan to link all thirteen colonies in a loose union. Although the colonists rejected this **Albany Plan**, it nevertheless represented one of the first steps toward a unified colonial America.

Identify the major reasons why England was able to
overcome tremendous early setbacks in exploring and
colonizing North America to eventually dominate the
continent.

Britain's success in exploring and colonizing North America hinged
on three factors: the determination and motivation of the
colonists, the rich resources and geographic features of the land
they settled, and the unique diversity of the settlers themselves.
These three factors gave Britain an advantage over competitors
and eventually led to England's domination of the continent.

The most significant reason for the success of Britain's
colonization efforts in North America was that British colonists
were simply more motivated to settle and create new homes and
lives in the New World than colonists from other countries. Many
Spanish and Portuguese colonists had only one primary goal:
making money, mainly through discovering gold. British colonists
wanted more than that. They wanted to start a new life. A sharp
population increase in the early seventeenth century throughout
Britain had resulted in an overcrowding of the major cities. This in
turn led to rampant disease and unemployment. The strict social
structure prohibited many of these poor and unemployed subjects
from moving above their current station as well. At the same time,
commercial organizations in the form of joint-stock companies
created a new economic engine that was constantly in search of
ways to generate profits through international exploration and
hardy souls willing to settle wild new lands. The combination of
these incentives gave England a distinct advantage over its
competitors.

The geography and natural resources of the land that Britain's
new colonies had inhabited also gave them the advantage over
other colonial efforts that had landed in less hospitable areas. The
plentiful woodlands provided the colonists with lumber with which
to build houses, and newly cleared fields offered fresh soil in
which to cultivate crops. Furthermore, the Native Americans
provided ample opportunities for trade. Exportable products like

Student Essay

tobacco, molasses, maize, beans, and potatoes not only supported the financial and physical investment of the farmers but also bolstered the growing merchant and banking classes in local towns. Thus, North America provided excellent opportunities to invest in a new life.

Unlike other countries that tried to establish colonies in the New World, the British colonists had diverse economic backgrounds, political views, religious convictions, as well as education and skills. While this meant that they often came into conflict with one another, they were generally able to settle their problems without violence. At times, this meant separation or isolation, but the overwhelming necessity for cooperation in order to survive in a strange land would eventually lead to the acceptance and tolerance of differing beliefs. This tolerance became a common feature of the settlers' culture and engendered a healthy spirit of competition. The colonies grew strong because of their diversity, planting the seeds for their eventual joint struggle for independence.

By the mid-eighteenth century, England had become the dominant imperial force in North America. Spain and Portugal had arrived in the New World long before the British and had already established trade and colonies on the African Coast, the Indies, and in Mexico. However, England had greater incentives to settle the New World. Furthermore, the bountiful resources of the lands it selected, as well as the diverse culture and hard work of its colonists, all helped to give Britain a decided advantage.

Test Questions and Answers

1. What were the differences between northern British colonies and southern British colonies?

- Most settlers in the northern colonies lived in townships centered around the local church, and religion played an extremely important role in their lives. Northerners generally farmed the land themselves. The North also developed an artisan class and engaged in manufacturing and banking.

- Southern settlers lived in relative isolation on large farms or plantations, producing labor-intensive crops like sugar, rice, and indigo. Slavery systems eventually developed in order to meet the demand for labor. Religion played only a small role in southerners' lives.

2. What roles did women play in the American colonies? How might this have made them victims in Salem witch trials?

- Women led isolated lives, confined to specific domestic roles, and women who ventured beyond these roles were distrusted or shunned.

- Women who did not follow the expected social patterns faced distrust and ostracization.

3. Explain the differences between the Puritans who settled in Plymouth and those who settled in Salem.

- The Puritans who settled Plymouth were Pilgrims, or Puritans who belonged to the most uncompromising sect. They were also known as Separatists because they believed that they needed to separate themselves completely from the Anglican Church.

- The Puritans at Salem were Reformists, not Separatists, and they believed that they could reform the Anglican Church from within.

Timeline

1692	Several people are tried and convicted of witchcraft in Salem, Massachusetts.
1699	Britain passes the Restraining Act to restrict manufacturing in the North American colonies.
1730–1740	The Great Awakening spreads a renewed spirit of evangelism throughout the American colonies.
1733	Britain passes the Molasses Act of 1733 to tax sugar and molasses imported into British colonies.
1739	British minister George Whitefield comes to North America from England to become a leading figure in the Great Awakening.
1741	Jonathan Edwards, a leading theologian, preaches his famous sermon, "Sinners in the Hands of an Angry God."
1750	Slavery is legalized in all thirteen colonies.
1755	French, English, Americans, and Native Americans begin fighting for control of North America in the French and Indian War.
1763	The Treaty of Paris ends the French and Indian War.

Major Figures

Jonathan Edwards An eighteenth-century theologian and philosopher, Edwards delivered rousing speeches throughout the American colonies during the Great Awakening to frighten colonists into worshipping God. Historians consider his most famous speech, "Sinners in the Hands of an Angry God," to be one of the most influential sermons in American history.

Benjamin Franklin A founding father and example of an Enlightened soul, Franklin ran a successful publishing company, published several scientific treatises, made significant advances in the field of science and medicine, and served as the U.S. ambassador to France during the Revolutionary War.

John Locke A philosopher of the Enlightenment, Locke theorized that people enter into contracts with their governments to ensure the protection of their natural rights. His ideas formed much of the intellectual backbone that justified the American Revolution.

George Washington A young lieutenant colonel in the Virginia militia, Washington started the French and Indian War when he attacked a small French garrison in the disputed Ohio Valley. He later helped lead American forces in the Revolutionary War against Britain and served as the first president of the United States.

George Whitefield A dynamic minister during the Great Awakening, Whitefield relied on dramatics to scare people into believing in God.

Suggested Reading

• Cooper, James Fenimore. *The Last of the Mohicans*. Reprint. West Berlin, New Jersey: Townsend Press, 2004.

Written in 1826, *The Last of the Mohicans* takes place during the French and Indian War. Lately, critics have criticized the book for its portrayal of the real events surrounding the Native American tribes and English and French armies at that time. However, the book is still an excellent and accurate portrayal of frontier life in 1750. A popular film of the book staring Daniel Day Lewis was released in 1992.

• Harms, Robert. *The Diligent: A Voyage Through the Worlds of the Slave Trade*. New York: Basic Books, 2003.

Yale historian Harms tells the story of the Atlantic slave trade by following the actions of one ship, the *Diligent*, which sailed in 1731. Harms relies on the journal of the ship's first lieutenant.

• Hill, Francis. *The Salem Witch Trials Reader*. New York: Da Capo Press, 2000.

This is a collection of first-hand accounts and testimonies about the Salem witch trials and their aftermath, with illuminating commentary.

Seeking Independence: 1763–1783

- Emergence of American Nationalism
- Resistance Becomes Rebellion
- The Revolution Begins
- Americans in Revolt
- Washington Wins the War

Prior to the French and Indian War, Britain had essentially left its American colonies to run themselves, a time often referred to as the age of "salutary neglect." Given relative freedom to do as they pleased, the North American settlers established unique forms of government to match their rugged sense of adventure and developing identity as Americans. But after the French and Indian War, Britain's relations with the colonies changed dramatically. Hoping to refill its empty treasury, Parliament levied more taxes on the Americans and tightened regulations governing trade.

Americans were outraged and offended at what they considered encroachments on their liberties. Over time, this indignation grew into a strong desire for rebellion. In just twelve years, between the end of the French and Indian War and the outbreak of the Revolutionary War, Americans transformed from loyal colonists into revolutionary patriots.

Emergence of American Nationalism

The American colonists were jubilant at the end of the French and Indian War in 1763, celebrating both their defeat of the French and the resulting access to the unexplored western frontier. With a new sense of confidence as they looked out across the vast and fertile new territory, Americans saw their future. But obstacles remained in the colonists' path as they sought to claim the land, and the freedom, that they believed was rightfully theirs.

PONTIAC'S REBELLION

Although Britain and the colonists had defeated the French and Native American forces in 1763, they continued to fight Native Americans along the western frontier for several more years. Many of the tribes in the Ohio Valley banded together under the leadership of Ottawa Chief **Pontiac**, a former ally of the French who resented American colonial encroachments on Indian lands.

By October, Pontiac's men had killed more than 2,000 British soldiers and American settlers and had destroyed all but three British outposts in the region. Pontiac eventually signed a peace treaty in 1766, but the British knew that more conflict would arise as long as colonial farmers kept pushing westward in search of new land.

> *Having lost the French and Indian War, Native American tribes hated the idea of having to deal with the aggressive and often arrogant, untrustworthy British. In contrast, the French had been respectful, did not try to remove them from their land, and did not pose a threat to the Native American way of life. Native Americans therefore called Pontiac's Uprising against the British the "War of National Liberation."*

The Proclamation of 1763

To prevent further bloodshed between whites and Indians, Britain issued the **Proclamation of 1763**, which prohibited colonists from settling west of the Appalachian Mountains. Only licensed trappers and traders would be allowed to venture farther, while those colonists who'd already settled beyond the mountains would have to relocate.

Although Britain had hoped the proclamation would help and protect Americans, most colonists were outraged at the policy, especially after they had shed so much blood during the war to win the land in the first place. In addition, many Americans believed that despite the proclamation, they had the right to expand westward. Feeling bitterly betrayed, many hardy colonists ignored the proclamation and crossed into the Ohio Valley anyway.

BRITISH WAR DEBT

Britain's victory in the French and Indian War had cost a fortune, nearly bankrupting the government. To refill the treasury and pay off debts owed to creditors, Prime Minister **George Grenville** convinced Parliamentarians to raise taxes both at home and in the colonies. Even though Britons paid significantly higher taxes than the Americans, colonists balked at the thought of higher taxes. They also resented **King George III**'s decision to permanently station 10,000 British regulars in North America to control his newly acquired territories.

The Sugar Act The first tax hike came in 1764 when Parliament passed the Sugar Act to tax molasses and other imports like textiles, wines, coffee, indigo and sugar. Colonists, of course, hated the Sugar Act because it was the first tax Parliament had ever levied on them solely to raise revenue.

The Currency Act Parliament also passed the Currency Act in 1764, which prohibited the colonists from printing their own cheap paper money. The Currency Act, combined with new taxes and stricter enforcement, shocked the American economy.

The Stamp Act Crisis of 1765 Although the Sugar and Currency Acts did increase revenue, Britain needed much more money in order to pay off war debts and keep troops posted in the colonies. To make up the difference, Grenville next proposed the Stamp Act to tax printed matter and legal documents in the colonies like newspapers, pamphlets, almanacs, bonds, licenses, deeds, diplomas, and even playing cards. Americans despised the Stamp Act more than the Sugar Act or the Currency Act because it taxed items they deemed necessities. More important, they also hated the tax because it challenged colonial assemblies' exclusive power to levy internal taxes.

Quartering Act Parliament passed the **Quartering Act** in 1765, forcing colonists to supply, feed, and house the unwanted British soldiers, even in their own homes if necessary. Colonists resented this act as a direct affront to their civil rights and personal liberties.

THE ISSUE OF REPRESENTATION

Many Americans protested under the cry of **"No taxation without representation!"** Prime Minister Grenville shot back that all members of Parliament represented the interests of all British subjects in the empire no matter where they lived. Colonial critics ridiculed this doctrine of **"virtual representation,"** believing that a small body of men could never satisfactorily represent people they knew nothing about.

> In reality, colonists didn't want representation in Parliament, because a few minor representatives in London would've been too politically weak to accomplish anything for the colonies. Rather, the slogan merely symbolized and explained the colonists' distaste for paying taxes they themselves hadn't legislated. Most believed that only locally elected legislatures had the right to levy taxes, not a government thousands of miles and an ocean away.

The Sons of Liberty

A group of educated colonists known as the **Sons of Liberty** began to hold meetings in public places under trees they dubbed "Liberty Trees" to discuss the Stamp Act and possible courses of action. They eventually organized a massive **Stamp Act Protest** in Boston in August 1765 and burned Boston's stamp agent in effigy as it swung from the city's Liberty Tree. Riotous mobs later destroyed the stamp office and ransacked the homes of the local customs officer and the royal governor, Thomas Hutchinson. Colonists also terrorized royal tax collectors to the point that many of the collectors fled the colonies to return to England.

BUILDING COLONIAL UNITY

Opposition to the Stamp Act united colonists, who initiated a widespread **boycott** of British goods in the hopes that desperate British manufacturers would pressure Parliament to repeal the tax. Mutual opposition to the Stamp Act also made colonists realize that they had more in common with each other than they did with Britons. To foster colonial unity, the Massachusetts House of Representatives issued a letter inviting the different colonial assemblies to a meeting. Nine of the colonies responded and sent delegates to New York to attend the **Stamp Act Congress** in October of 1765.

The twenty-seven men who gathered at the congress registered their complaints in the **Declaration of the Rights and Grievances of the Colonies**, petitioning King George III and Parliament to repeal the Stamp Act. Under pressure from British manufacturers and unwilling to enforce the collection of an incredibly unpopular tax, Parliament ultimately consented and repealed the Stamp Act. At the same time, however, it quietly passed the **Declaratory Act**, asserting Parliament's right to tax the colonies in "all cases whatsoever." The Declaratory Act allowed Parliament to save face and provided a temporary solution to the brewing crisis.

CHAPTER 3
1763–1783

Resistance Becomes Rebellion

In 1767, Parliament passed the **Townshend Acts**, which levied taxes on virtually all imports entering the colonies from Great Britain. Although the taxes did increase revenue, they sparked another round of fiery protests from the colonists.

SAMUEL ADAMS FUELS THE REVOLUTION

The ardent Bostonian revolutionary and Son of Liberty **Samuel Adams** launched a citywide propaganda campaign to protest the Townshend taxes. He distributed pamphlets, letters, and essays on the injustices of British rule, all of which quickly spread throughout the colonies. Within just a few years, colonists in most every major city and town from the South to New England had formed their own campaigns.

THE BOSTON MASSACRE

Bostonians hated royal encroachments on colonial liberties, and took their resentment out on the British soldiers garrisoned in the city. Crowds taunted and jeered at the troops for months until the tense situation finally exploded. On March 5, 1770, several British soldiers fired into a crowd of rock-throwing colonists, killing five Bostonians. News of the **Boston Massacre** spread rapidly through the colonies. Hoping to avoid further bloodshed, Parliament repealed all the Townshend duties except for the tax on tea, mostly as a symbol of royal authority.

TAXING TEA

The new Prime Minister, Frederick Lord North, eventually, even drastically, reduced this last tax on tea in order to help the failing East India Company unload its surplus of tea. North also believed that the tax reduction would appease the Americans and restore good relations between Britain and the colonies. Yet colonists resented the reduced tax because they believed it was a British trick to bribe the colonies, grant a monopoly to the East India Company, and ultimately control all colonial trade. Many worried that if Britain successfully regulated the tea trade, they might also try to control other commodities in the future.

> *Colonists hated the tax on tea because most considered it an essential for daily, civilized life. While other taxes imposed by Parliament, like those on sugar and stamps, only affected a few segments of society, the tax on tea affected everyone.*

THE BOSTON TEA PARTY

Rebels like Sam Adams churned out more propaganda in response to the reduced tax and urged colonists to boycott tea. Port officials throughout the colonies refused to allow East India Company tea ships to unload their cargoes, forcing them to sail back to England. In Boston, however, Governor Hutchinson wouldn't allow the tea ships to return, either, forcing them to remain in port.

The Bostonian Sons of Liberty ended the stalemate on the night of December 16, 1773, when, disguised as Mohawk Indians, they boarded the tea ships and threw several hundred chests of tea into the harbor. Several hundred spectators watched the **Boston Tea Party** unfold and wondered how Britain would respond to such blatant defiance of royal authority.

THE INTOLERABLE COERCIVE ACTS

Outraged, King George III and Parliament immediately passed the **Coercive Acts** to punish Bostonians and exact payment for the thousands of pounds of lost tea. These acts included:

- **The Boston Port Act**, which closed Boston Harbor until the city had repaid the East India Company for the tea. The act paralyzed Boston's maritime economy.

- A new **Quartering Act** requiring Bostonians to house and feed several thousand British soldiers sent to enforce the Coercive Acts.

- **The Massachusetts Government Act**, which cancelled city elections and indefinitely closed town meetings.

Britain hoped their harsh punishment would make an example of Boston and convince Americans in the other colonies to obey the Crown in the future. Instead, the Coercive Acts fostered a greater sense of unity among the thirteen colonies because many thought the punishment too great for the crime. Colonists everywhere rallied to Boston's aid, delivering food and winter supplies from as far away as Georgia.

> Colonists called the Coercive Acts the **"Intolerable Acts"** because they found the new restrictions so unbearable. While taxes on sugar, stamps, and tea were one thing, the closing of a port and invasion of colonial homes was something quite different. The acts directly led the colonists from thoughts of rebellion to the actual planning of an insurrection.

CHAPTER 3
1763–1783

British Acts and Colonial Response

British Act	Colonial Response
Writs of Assistance, 1760	Challenged laws in Massachusetts Supreme Court, lost case
Sugar Act, 1764	Weak protest by colonial legislatures
Stamp Act, 1765	Virginia Resolves, mobs, Sons of Liberty, Stamp Act Congress
Townshend Duties, 1767	*Letters from a Pennsylvania Farmer*, boycott, Boston Massacre
Tea Act, 1773	Boston Tea Party
Intolerable Acts, 1773	First Continental Congress

THE FIRST CONTINENTAL CONGRESS

Most colonial leaders agreed that the Coercive Acts required a unified response from all of the colonies. Twelve colonies (Georgia abstaining) sent a total of fifty-five delegates to the **First Continental Congress** in Philadelphia in 1774 to draft an official protest. A few of the delegates hoped the Congress would become a colonial parliament of sorts, and proposed measures that would lead to colonial government, but the majority rejected their proposals. Most delegates wanted Congress only to resolve the brewing crisis in Boston, not establish a colonial government or start a rebellion.

Declaration of American Rights

Delegates at the First Continental Congress drafted the **Declaration of American Rights** in 1774, which declared Parliament had no authority over internal colonial affairs. They also created the **Continental Association** to coordinate a stricter boycott on all British goods throughout the colonies. Association committees eventually became the backbone of the Revolution.

An infuriated King George III heard of the colonial meeting and Declaration of American Rights and remarked, "New England colonies are in a state of rebellion," and that "blows must decide whether they are to be subject to this country or independent."

The Revolution Begins

By 1775, resentment toward Britain had calcified into the desire for rebellion. Many cities and towns organized volunteer militias that drilled openly in public common areas while King George III grew increasingly intolerant of American resistance to royal authority.

LEXINGTON AND CONCORD

On April 15, 1775, a British commander dispatched troops to arrest Samuel Adams and John Hancock and seize the arsenal of weapons cached in Concord, Massachusetts. Militiamen from nearby Lexington intercepted them and opened fire. Eight Americans died as the British sliced through the line and moved on to Concord. The **redcoats** arrived in Concord, however, only to find the Concord militia waiting for them. Militiamen fired their muskets from the protection of the forest trees and stone walls into the organized columns of bright red uniforms, killing seventy British soldiers and forcing the British to retreat back to Boston.

> *Colonial militiamen were often referred to as "minutemen" for their supposed ability to dress and prepare for battle in under sixty seconds. Bostonian silversmith and Son of Liberty* **Paul Revere** *made his famous "Midnight Ride" on April 14, 1775, from Boston to Lexington and Concord to warn the minutemen of the redcoats' approach.*

THE SECOND CONTINENTAL CONGRESS

Almost immediately after the **Battle of Lexington and Concord**, thousands of militiamen surrounded Boston to prevent the British troops from leaving. Meanwhile, delegates from all thirteen colonies gathered once again in Philadelphia at the **Second Continental Congress** to discuss the battle and its consequences. Because most delegates still desired reconciliation with King George III and Parliament, they agreed to sign a petition professing their love for King George III in a document called the **Olive Branch Petition**. They beseeched the king to recall the troops in Boston to restore peace between the colonies and Britain. King George III ultimately rejected the petition. After the British defeat at the Battle of Bunker Hill, King George III officially declared the colonies in a state of rebellion. Any hope of reconciliation and a return to the pre-1763 status quo had vanished.

Washington Takes Command

Even though delegates at the Second Continental Congress had signed the Olive Branch Petition, they also agreed to bolster colonial defenses in case of war. They set aside funds to organize an army and a small navy and also selected **George Washington** to command the newly christened **Continental Army** surrounding Boston.

While all colonists now believed that their rights had been infringed upon and were ready for action, many feared that not all colonies would support armed revolution, especially those in the South. The delegates hoped that Washington's stature as a highly respected Virginian plantation owner would further unite the northern and southern colonies.

INDEPENDENCE

Their Olive Branch petition rejected, delegates at the Second Continental Congress finally elected to declare independence from Britain on July 2, 1776. They then selected **Thomas Jefferson** to draft the congress's official **Declaration of Independence**.

Life, Liberty, and the Pursuit of Happiness

Jefferson kept the Declaration relatively short because he wanted it to be direct, clear, and forceful. He wrote:

> **We hold these truths to be self-evident, that all men are created equal, that they are endowed by their Creator with certain unalienable rights, that among these are Life, Liberty, and the pursuit of Happiness.**

Drawing from the writings of John Locke, Jefferson argued that governments exist in order to protect the rights of the people, and that the people have a right and even a duty to overthrow governments that fail their mandate.

A Long Train of Abuses

Jefferson further justified the Revolution by detailing King George III's "abuses and usurpations" against the American colonies, including:

- Shutting down representative colonial legislatures
- Refusing to allow the colonies to govern themselves
- Assuming judicial powers and manipulating the court system
- Conspiring with Native Americans against the colonists
- Restricting trade
- Imposing unjust taxes
- Coercing American sailors to work on British ships
- Taking military actions against Americans
- Refusing to allow colonists to redress grievances

Jefferson argued that the colonists should establish a new government as the United States of America in order to protect their rights.

> *John Locke's* Second Treatise of Civil Government *had an enormous impact on the thought of American revolutionaries. The foundation of Locke's theories lay in the belief that all people had natural and irrevocable rights to life, liberty, and property, and that governments existed solely to protect those rights. Consequently, if the government violated its contract with the people, then the people had the right to rebel and establish a better government.*

Americans in Revolt

All thirteen colonies immediately prepared for war after the Battle of Lexington and Concord. New militias formed throughout America, usually for the sole purpose of defending local communities from British aggression. Other units, however, rushed to join their comrades, who were cornered by British troops in Boston. Under the

CHAPTER 3
1763–1783

strict command of George Washington, Nathaniel Greene, and the German Baron von Steuben, this ragtag collection of undisciplined militiamen eventually became the well-trained **Continental Army**.

> Historians estimate that approximately 350,000 soldiers, or two-thirds of eligible American men in the colonies, served in the Continental Army, local militias, or a combination of both during the Revolutionary War.

COMMON SENSE

The radical English author and philosopher **Thomas Paine** helped turn American public opinion against Great Britain and solidify the emerging colonial unity. In January 1776, he published *Common Sense*, a pamphlet that denounced King George III as a tyrannical "brute." He called on Americans to unite and overthrow British rule so that they could usher in an era of freedom for humanity. Within only a few months of its first printing, Americans had purchased more than 100,000 copies of the pamphlet.

WOMEN IN THE WAR

Most American women supported the war effort as well. Some particularly daring women chose to serve as nurses, attendants, cooks, spies, and even as combatants on the battlefields. The majority of women, however, fought the war at home by managing the family farms and businesses. Making yarn and homespun necessities like socks and underwear to send to militiamen and supporting the boycott on British goods were significant contributions by female Americans.

Sadly, the Founding Fathers never recognized women's tremendous wartime efforts. Despite Abigail Adams's private plea to her husband, John Adams, to "remember the ladies" when making new laws, women didn't receive the right to vote or to even own property at war's end.

THE LOYALISTS

Although most Americans supported the decision to break away from Great Britain and declare independence, about one-fifth of the colonists chose to remain loyal to the Crown. Some, including many lawyers, Anglican clergymen, and royal officials felt that challenging British rule was unconscionable, while others simply wished to maintain the status quo. Although **Loyalists** lived throughout America, the majority lived in the lower southern colonies. Over 100,000 Loyalists fled to Canada, England, and the West Indies before and during the war. Loyalists who stayed in the colonies faced persecution and even death.

NATIVE AMERICANS

Most Native Americans were particularly afraid of future American expansion onto their lands and therefore sided with Great Britain in the war. The influential Mohawk chief **Joseph Brant**, for example, successfully convinced the Iroquois, Creek, Cherokees, and Choctaw, among others, to raid American settlements and outposts in the West.

AFRICAN AMERICANS

Blacks generally supported the British because an American victory would only keep them enslaved. Although approximately 5,000 blacks did serve in militias for the United States, most fled to British encampments and Loyalist areas to escape bondage. As a result, both northern and southern colonies lost tens of thousands of slaves during the war. Those blacks who didn't have the opportunity to escape remained enslaved despite Jefferson's belief that "all men were created equal."

THE UNDECIDED

Finally, some men and women neither supported nor opposed the revolution and opted instead to wait and see what would happen. Because civilian casualties remained low throughout the war, sitting on the fence proved to be a good alternative to fighting for those who didn't much care which side won or lost. Patriotic colonies often tried to reduce the number of free riders by passing laws that essentially ordered, "you're either with us or against us," and many townships prosecuted able-bodied men who failed to join militias.

Washington Wins the War

The odds stood in favor of the British at the beginning of the war since they had the world's most powerful navy, a huge standing army in North America, and a large force of German Hessian mercenaries ready to fight. They soon discovered, however, that fighting in North America was exceedingly difficult. Though George Washington had to rely on a small, inconsistent volunteer force, he could also rely on local militias that used hit-and-run guerilla tactics to confuse the orderly columns of British regulars.

Washington wisely understood that he only needed to outlast the British—not defeat them in every engagement. He knew that Britain would eventually grow tired of fighting an unpopular war so far away from home. Washington focused primarily on outrunning the British, forcing his adversary to chase his Continental Army from colony to colony. This tactic worked brilliantly, considering the Americans didn't have any key strategic areas they needed to defend.

BATTLE OF SARATOGA

The first military success for the colonists came at **Saratoga** in upstate New York in October 1777, when more than 5,700 British troops surrendered to American forces. This victory turned the war around for the Americans because it demonstrated to France that Britain might actually lose the war. By the following year, the two sides had formed the **Franco-American alliance** and agreed to fight the British together until the United States achieved independence.

FRENCH INTERVENTION

Many historians believe that the colonists could not have won the war without French assistance. France, for example, sent fresh troops and supplies to North America to take pressure off the out-numbered Continental Army. More important, however, France's participation expanded the scope of the war. Before long, Britain found itself pitted against the Spanish and the Dutch as well as the French and the Americans and fighting battles in North America, Europe, the Mediterranean, Africa, India, and the West Indies.

BATTLE OF YORKTOWN

Washington, meanwhile, continued to engage the British in North America, first in a series of western campaigns and then in Georgia and South Carolina. Eventually, he moved back north-ward to join French forces surrounding Britain's General Corn-wallis at **Yorktown**, Virginia. Cornered and greatly outnumbered, Cornwallis surrendered to Washington on Octo-ber 19, 1781, and thus ended the Revolutionary War.

THE TREATY OF PARIS

Once the fighting had stopped, the Continental Congress sent John Adams, John Jay, and Benjamin Franklin to negotiate a per-manent settlement. They eventually signed the Treaty of Paris on September 3, 1783, in which Great Britain recognized the United States as an independent nation and established a western border along the Mississippi River. The last British troops left New York, and the Continental Army disbanded.

CHAPTER 3
1763–1783

Americans were still professing their love for King George III and a desire for peaceful reconciliation as late as 1775, and had Britain accepted the Second Continental Congress's Olive Branch Petition, the Revolutionary War could have been avoided. Support or refute this claim using historical evidence.

Even if Britain had accepted the Second Continental Congress's Olive Branch Petition, a war between the thirteen colonies and Great Britain would have been difficult to avoid. Though the delegates at the Congress expected to heal the rift with Britain, public opinion held an entirely different view of the matter. An ongoing economic struggle against British taxation since the end of the French and Indian War in 1763 had convinced the colonial population that their resistance was both necessary and effective. In addition, colonial governments, not Parliament, had been recognized by the colonists for many years as the law of the land, and colonists were outraged when King George III tried to exert power over these assemblies. Then, on April 19, 1775, British forces traded shots with colonial rebels at Lexington and Concord, and more than 100 men lay dead. The public was enraged, and the rapid spread of anti-British propaganda helped to fan the flames. There seemed little that could stop armed revolt, a fact that the Second Continental Congress itself recognized as demonstrated by their final actions of the meeting. Despite the Olive Branch Petition and the delegates' professed love for King George III, the Revolutionary War was all but inevitable.

At the heart of the dispute was a staunch economic struggle between the colonies and the British government, which saw the colonies primarily as a source of revenue. England was having severe financial difficulties by 1763, the end of the French and Indian War, and sought to squeeze the American colonies for additional funds by enacting new taxes. These taxes included the Stamp Act of 1765, which was basically a sales tax on a variety of goods and services, including those produced locally in the colonies. Still other taxes were placed upon imported goods, ultimately culminating in a colonial boycott on all British goods

Student Essay

and a series of revolts against the taxes, including the famous
Boston Tea Party. During this period, increasing numbers of
British soldiers were deployed to the colonies to put down the
insurrections. However, Britain had vastly underestimated the
resourcefulness of the colonists, as well as the degree of their
discontent.

To make matters worse for Britain, the Crown's actions in the
colonies had been well documented by a resistance group known
as the Committees of Correspondence. By 1775, they had begun
distributing anti-British propaganda detailing England's crimes
against the colonies in pamphlets and newspapers from Georgia to
Boston. These materials were widely read by city dwellers and
rural settlers alike, and the colonists were furious at having the
fruits of their labor taxed by a power that offered them very little
in return. When British soldiers left Boston for Lexington to seize
what they considered to be "rebel" supplies, a collection of
farmers organized into a small militia and stood waiting for them
on the village green. When a shot rang out, the British regulars
fired upon the militia, leaving eight colonists dead. The public's
outrage could no longer be contained.

There was also the mentality of the colonists to consider. For
years they had been left alone to fend for themselves in a new and
sometimes hostile world, thousands of miles away from England
and Parliament. They had created their own governments with
little help from the Crown, assemblies that were led and run by
colonists. Colonists had grown to recognize these local
governments as the law of the land, even before the King and
Parliament. When representatives from England overruled these
governments, specifically with the Coercive (Intolerable) Acts,
which restructured the Massachusetts government and restricted

town meetings, colonists felt that their rights had been disregarded, which only added fuel to the fire.

The Second Continental Congress, which first met on May 10, 1775, was called in direct response to the events at Lexington and Concord. Delegates from every colony met in Philadelphia, and the Congress began with the assumption that the rift between the colonies and England could be healed. The delegates elected to send an "Olive Branch Petition" to King George III, pledging loyalty to the Crown and requesting a cease-fire. However, the delegates themselves also demonstrated a basic understanding of the improbability of reconciliation. Even as they signed their names to the Olive Branch Petition, the delegates also made provisions to organize both a navy and an army in preparation for a possible military conflict.

Thoughts of independence had turned to action in a way that could not be undone. This was proven at the Battles of Lexington and Concord, and later at Bunker Hill, where another militia of farmers refused to retreat from the large and intimidating British Army. Years of unfair taxation had taken their toll. Colonial leaders felt justified in their resistance, and had generated wide support through an effective propaganda campaign. Although the delegates of the Second Continental Congress were petitioning for peace, it is clear they were doubtful that a peaceful solution could be found. Fending for themselves for so long in a far-away land had changed the colonists; they had evolved from British subjects into American patriots.

Test Questions and Answers

1. How did the French and Indian War affect British colonial policy?

- Britain created a unified colonial policy for the first time.

- Britain increased colonial taxes to pay for the war.

- Britain permanently stationed troops in North America to protect colonists from Native Americans.

- Britain issued the Proclamation of 1763 to prevent colonists from settling west of the Appalachians.

2. What was the purpose of the Stamp Act?

- Parliament passed the act to help pay for British soldiers stationed in the colonies.

- The tax also helped pay off debts incurred during the French and Indian War.

3. What did Americans mean by, "No taxation without representation"?

- Colonists used this as a rallying cry to protest unpopular taxes created by the Sugar Act, the Stamp Act, and later the Townshend Acts.

- This statement captures the colonists' love of representative governments.

- The statement rejects the concept of "virtual representation."

- This served as a symbolic rallying cry, because colonists didn't seriously want representation in British Parliament.

4. Did the 1765 Stamp Act or the 1766 Declaratory Act have a more profound impact on American anti-British sentiment?

- The Declaratory Act had a more profound impact on anti-British sentiment because Parliament used it to justify all future legislation regarding the colonies.

- Colonists hated the Stamp Act, but kept resistance short of outright rebellion.

- Parliament used it to justify the Townshend Acts and the Intolerable Acts, both of which brought the colonists much closer to war than the Stamp Act ever had.

Timeline

1763	Peace of Paris ends French and Indian War.
	Pontiac's Rebellion occurs.
	Parliament issues the Proclamation of 1763.
1764	Parliament passes the Sugar and Currency Acts.
1765	Parliament passes the Quartering and Stamp Acts.
	The Stamp Act Congress convenes in New York.
	Stamp Act riots and protests spread throughout colonies.
1766	Parliament repeals the Stamp Act and passes the Declaratory Act.
1767	Parliament passes the Townshend Acts and suspends the New York legislature.
1768	British soldiers occupy Boston.
1770	Boston Massacre occurs.
	Parliament repeals Townshend Acts but keeps the tax on tea.
1772	Samuel Adams forms the committee of correspondence.
1773	Boston Tea Party occurs.
1774	Parliament passes the Coercive or "Intolerable" Acts.
	The First Continental Congress convenes and drafts the Declaration of American Rights.
1775	Battle of Lexington and Concord occurs.
	The Second Continental Congress convenes.
	Battle of Bunker Hill occurs.
	Paul Revere warns minutemen of redcoats' approach in his Midnight Ride.
1776	Thomas Paine writes *Common Sense*.
	Congress votes for independence; Thomas Jefferson writes the Declaration of Independence.
1777	Battle of Saratoga brings first military success for the colonists.
1778	France and the United States form the Franco-American alliance.
1781	Washington accepts Cornwallis' surrender at Yorktown.
1783	The Treaty of Paris ends the Revolutionary War.

Major Figures

Samuel Adams Cousin to John Adams, Adams was a failed Bostonian businessman who became an ardent political activist in the years leading up to the Revolutionary War. He organized the first Committee of Correspondence and was a delegate to both Continental Congresses in 1774 and 1775.

Joseph Brant A Mohawk chief and influential leader of the Iroquois tribes, Brant was one of the many Native American leaders who advocated an alliance with Britain against the Americans in the Revolutionary War. Although he had no love for the British, he and other tribe leaders feared the land-hungry American settlers even more.

George Grenville Prime Minister of Parliament at the close of the French and Indian War, Grenville was responsible for enforcing the Navigation Laws and passing the Sugar, Stamp, Currency, and Quartering Acts in the mid-1760s. He wrongly assumed that colonists would be willing to bear a greater tax burden after Britain had invested so much in protecting them from the French and Native Americans in the previous decade.

Thomas Jefferson A Virginian planter and lawyer, Jefferson was invaluable to the revolutionary cause. He drafted the Declaration of Independence in 1776, which justified American independence from Great Britain. Later, he served as the first secretary of state under President George Washington and as vice president to John Adams. He was elected president in 1800 and 1804.

King George III Having inherited his father's throne at the young age of twelve, George III was King of Great Britain throughout the French and Indian War (the Seven Years' War), the American Revolutionary War, the Napoleonic Wars, and the War of 1812. After the conclusion of the French and Indian War, his popularity steadily declined in the American colonies. In the Declaration of Independence, Thomas Jefferson vilifies George III and argues that his neglect and misuse of the American colonies justified their revolution.

Thomas Paine An exile from England, Paine was a radical philosopher who supported republicanism and civic virtue. His 1776 pamphlet *Common Sense* was a bestselling phenomenon in the American colonies and convinced thousands to rebel against the "royal brute" King George III.

Pontiac An Ottowa chief, Pontiac was disillusioned by the French defeat in the French and Indian War. Pontiac briefly united various tribes in the Ohio and Mississippi Valleys to raid colonists on the western frontiers of British North America from 1763–1766. He was eventually killed by another Native American after the British had crushed his uprising. Parliament issued the Proclamation of 1763 to prevent any future tribal insurrections against British colonists.

George Washington A young Virginia planter and militia officer, Washington served in the French and Indian War in 1754. He later became commander in chief of the American forces during the Revolutionary War and first president of the United States in 1789. Although he lost most of the battles he fought, his leadership skills were unparalleled and were integral to the creation of the United States.

CHAPTER 3
1763–1783

Suggested Reading

- Cook, Don. *The Long Fuse: How England Lost the American Colonies, 1760–1785*. Boston: Atlantic Monthly Press, 1996.

Another account of the Revolutionary War period in American history from the British side, *The Long Fuse* features significant information on Benjamin Franklin and his efforts on behalf of the colonists.

- Martin, Joseph Plumb. *A Narrative of a Revolutionary Soldier: Some of the Adventures, Dangers, and Sufferings of Joseph Plumb Martin*. New York: Signet Classic Edition, 2001.

This book reveals the Revolutionary War through the eyes of a soldier in Washington's Continental Army. Martin's diary is rich with accounts of the daily life of a soldier, but light on the actual battles themselves.

- Peason, Michael. *Those Damned Rebels: The American Revolution as Seen Through British Eyes*. New York: Da Capo Press, 2000.

Originally published in 1972 and rereleased in 2000, this work relays the British perspective on the American Revolution, using journals, letters, diaries, and field reports to give a first-hand glimpse of how Britons regarded their fellow countrymen in the New World.

Building a Nation: 1781–1800

- The Articles of Confederation
- Forming a More Perfect Union
- Ratifying the Constitution
- Washington's Presidency
- Adams and the Federalists

4

Shortly after Thomas Jefferson penned the Declaration of Independence, the delegates at the Second Continental Congress drafted the Articles of Confederation, the first constitution of the United States. The Articles, however, failed to truly bind the states together, and as a result, the congress had very little real power. Less than a decade later, congressional leaders decided to scrap the Articles in favor of creating a new and stronger federal government.

Political philosophers around the world have hailed the Constitution as one of the most important documents in world history. It established the first stable democratic government and inspired the creation of similar constitutions around the world. For this reason, past historians have waxed lyrical about the Founding Fathers' incredible foresight when writing the Constitution. Many contemporary historians, however, tend to see the Constitution more as a bundle of compromises rather than a document they knew would change the world. Either way, the Constitution established a much stronger federal government and has since become the oldest living written constitution in the world.

The Articles of Confederation

Delegates at the Second Continental Congress drafted the **Articles of Confederation** to create the first national government of the United States. The Articles loosely bound the thirteen states in a confederacy that eventually proved incredibly weak.

A WEAK NATIONAL GOVERNMENT

Wary of strong central governments after their interactions with Britain, delegates at the Second Continental Congress made certain that the new national congress created under the Articles of Confederation would have very little authority over state legislatures. Instead, drafters hoped that the congress would act as a collective substitute for a monarch, or a multiperson executive. The Articles stipulated that the Congress could do the following:

- Negotiate treaties, declare war, and make peace

- Coin money

- Issue loans

- Maintain an army and a navy

- Operate a postal service

- Negotiate treaties with Native Americans

- Resolve disputes among the states

- Govern western territories for the benefit of all states

The Articles clearly stated that the individual states reserved all powers not specifically granted to congress. Representative governments in the states would levy their own taxes, for example, and then use a percentage of the duties collected to pay their share of national expenditures. Over time, this unfolded as an ineffective way of bankrolling a federal government, primarily because many of the states refused to pay their fair share.

Moreover, Congress had been granted no rights to control interstate commerce. States were thus given a free hand to draft conflicting and confusing laws that made trade across borders difficult. Finally, any changes to the Articles of Confederation required unanimous agreement from all states in the Union, an event that was unlikely to occur even on the smallest issue.

GOVERNING WESTERN LANDS

After the Articles of Confederation went into effect, Congress passed two landmark laws to govern American territories in the West:

- **The Land Ordinance of 1785**, which helped the government survey western lands. The law created townships, each six miles square, that were divided into thirty-six square-mile sections and auctioned to the highest bidder so that any American could settle in the West.

- **The Northwest Ordinance of 1787**, which stipulated that a western territory could apply for full statehood as soon as it had the same number of people as the least populous of the original thirteen states. The ordinance made certain that new states would receive equal footing with older states and that all citizens of the territories would have the same rights as the citizens of the states.

CONTINENTAL DOLLARS AND DEPRESSION

The new Congress immediately set to printing paper currency in order to pay for the Revolutionary War. The money became the standard currency in the United States during the war, but when hard times hit and inflation skyrocketed, these Continental dollars became "not worth a Continental." Many Americans, especially farmers, faced hardship as the economy slid into depression. Congress requested that states increase taxes to help pay for a new national currency, but most states refused and printed their own paper money instead. This, too, quickly succumbed to inflation, and by the end of the war Americans had fistfuls of a variety of worthless money.

Shays's Rebellion

Frustration with the economic depression boiled over in 1786. Farmers throughout the colonies were suffering intensely after the revolution, mainly due to the worthless Continentals they were forced to use as money. Most of the state legislatures refused to provide any assistance to these impoverished farmers and, in some cases, even raised taxes. Unable to find any relief, and still intoxicated from their success in the Revolution, many farmers grabbed their muskets once again and marched on the various state capitals to demand new governments.

The most notorious of these small uprising was **Shays's Rebellion**. Led by the Revolutionary war hero **Daniel Shays**, protesters attacked Massachusetts's courthouses to prevent local judges from foreclosing on farms. The state legislature ultimately used militia troops to crush the uprising. Still, Shays's Rebellion awakened legislators in Massachusetts and throughout the states to the inadequacies of the existing political system.

Forming a More Perfect Union

With Congress's permission, delegates met in Annapolis, Maryland, in 1786 and again in Philadelphia in 1787 to discuss revising the Articles of Confederation. The delegates, however, soon realized that the Articles needed to be scrapped entirely to create a stronger central government.

> Although Shays's Rebellion had certainly prompted many Americans to question the effectiveness of the federal government, leaders ultimately decided the Articles of Confederation needed amending primarily because the national congress had no power to control interstate commerce or interstate disputes. States' rights versus the power of the federal government would be an issue throughout the next century in the United States.

THE FRAMERS

The fifty-five men who gathered at the **Constitutional Convention** in Philadelphia came from the upper echelons of society. Most had attended college and had become wealthy planters, lawyers, and merchants but generally understood that they served all classes of Americans. On the other hand, the delegates did want the new government to protect individuals' rights to acquire and hold wealth.

Interestingly, most all of the attendees had not been heavily involved in the revolution: **Thomas Jefferson**, **John Adams**, Samuel Adams, and Patrick Henry were all absent. Nevertheless, most did have experience writing their own state constitutions. Delegates unanimously selected **George Washington** to chair the convention.

CREATING A NEW GOVERNMENT

The men gathered in Philadelphia quickly realized the Articles of Confederation should be scrapped and replaced with a new constitution to create a stronger national government. Even though this decision violated Congress's mandate to merely *revise* the Articles, most delegates feared the Union would collapse without a stronger central government. The delegates drafted a new **Constitution** to create a republican government consisting of three distinct branches: a legislative branch (Congress), an executive branch (the president), and a judicial branch (headed by the Supreme Court). The delegates felt that this **separation of powers** into three different branches would prevent tyranny over the states.

VIRGINIA VS. NEW JERSEY

Both Virginia and New Jersey submitted proposals for a new national legislature, plans that divided delegates and nearly deadlocked the convention. The **Virginia Plan** called for the creation of a bicameral national legislature, or a new Congress with an upper and lower house, in which the number of representatives per state would be apportioned based on that state's population. Many of the more populous states supported this **"large state plan"** because it would give them more power.

New Jersey, on the other hand, proposed the creation of a unicameral legislature in which all states large and small would have the same number of representatives. This **"small state plan"** or **New Jersey Plan**, would have tipped the balance of power to favor the smaller states over the larger ones.

The framers of the constitution did not create a true democracy, which would have been based only on a popular vote, because they didn't trust the "rabble" of uneducated commoners. Instead, they created a republic, a system based on the consent of the governed, where representatives exercised power for the public.

The Great Compromise

Eventually, the delegates settled on a **"Great Compromise"** to please both Virginia and New Jersey. They decided that the new Congress would have two houses, a Senate in which all states would be equally represented by two senators, and a lower House of Representatives in which the number of delegates would be apportioned based on state population. State legislatures would appoint senators every six years, while the people would elect representatives to the House every two years. The new congress retained all the powers it had under the Articles of Confederation but also had the power to levy taxes.

The Three-Fifths Compromise

Even at this early date, the slavery issue divided the northern and southern states. States with large slave populations wanted slaves to count as people on the official census so that they could have more representatives in the House. States with smaller populations wanted to exclude slaves altogether. Delegates finally made the so-called **Three-fifths Compromise** to count slaves as three-fifths of a person. They also agreed to discuss banning the slave trade in 1808.

THE PRESIDENCY

After they had created the legislative branch, the delegates moved on to creating a strong executive branch. Most agreed that the Articles of Confederation had left Congress too weak to maintain unity among all thirteen states. To amend this, delegates outlined the powers of a new executive or president of the United States. Elected to a term of four years, the president had the following authority:

• To serve as commander in chief of the army and navy

- To appoint judges to all federal courts
- To veto legislation passed by Congress

Just as important, the House of Representatives could also impeach the president for treason, bribery, and other "high crimes and misdemeanors," because the delegates wanted to make sure the president never became a king.

> Some delegates, such as **Alexander Hamilton**, officially proposed creating a constitutional monarchy headed by an American king. Although few supported his proposal, many delegates agreed that a strong executive would be necessary to maintain stability.

THE ELECTORAL COLLEGE

Fearing that the democratic "rabble" would elect an uneducated man to the presidency, the Constitution's framers stipulated that the people would only indirectly elect presidents. Instead, state legislatures would choose a select body of educated men to cast the final votes for the president in the **Electoral College**.

In theory, voters in the college would vote according to the outcome of the popular vote in their states; however, should the people elect a person deemed unqualified for the presidency, electoral voters could change the vote to ensure that only the "best man" become president.

THE JUDICIARY

Finally, the delegates turned to creating a judicial branch. They created a system of federal circuit courts headed by a Supreme Court that outranked all other courts in the nation. The Senate had to approve of all presidential appointments to the Supreme Court, particularly since justices would serve life terms. The Constitution also stipulated that Congress's first duty would be to create the federal court system.

CHECKS AND BALANCES

Despite separation of powers, most delegates wanted to include other safeguards in the Constitution to prevent tyranny. They therefore created a system of **checks and balances** so that each branch of government had the ability to check the powers of the others in order to prevent one branch from dominating the others. The president, for example, has the right to appoint Supreme Court justices, cabinet members, and foreign ambassadors, but only with the approval of the Senate. On the other hand, he reserves the right to veto all congressional legislation. Congress, too, could override a presidential veto with a two-thirds majority vote.

> *Separation of powers and checks and balance were truly revolutionary. Up to this point in history, government had mainly been composed of single ruling monarchs who decided what was best for their country. This monarch's rule was law, unchecked and without question. Never before had anyone proposed controlling government by setting it against itself, as the Americans proposed with the checks and balances system.*

Ratifying the Constitution

Even though the delegates at the Constitutional Convention in Philadelphia had succeeded in drafting a new Constitution to replace the Articles of Confederation, they still had to convince state legislatures to approve the radically different document.

The Articles of Confederation stipulated that all thirteen states must unanimously ratify the Constitution in order for it to take effect. To circumvent this undoubtedly impossible task, the Philadelphia delegates included in the Constitution a section outlining a new plan for ratification. When only nine of the states ratified the document at special conventions with elected representatives, the Constitution would replace the Articles in those nine states. The delegates figured correctly that the remaining states would be unable to survive on their own and would therefore have to ratify the Constitution as well. In effect, the framers of the Constitution chose to appeal to the American people to ensure ratification.

FEDERALISTS VS. ANTI-FEDERALISTS

Debates immediately erupted throughout the thirteen states as to whether or not the new Constitution should replace the Articles of Confederation. The Federalists, or those who supported ratification, generally came from the more educated and wealthier classes and included leaders like John Adams, George Washington, Benjamin Franklin, **James Madison**, and **Alexander Hamilton**, among others.

The Anti-Federalists favored a weaker central government in favor of stronger state legislatures. Not all of them liked the Articles of Confederation, but none of them wanted the new Constitution either. Generally from the poorer classes in the West, but also with the support of patriots like Samuel Adams and Patrick Henry, the Anti-Federalists feared that a stronger national government would one day destroy the liberties Americans had won in the Revolutionary War. They particularly didn't like the fact that the new Constitution didn't delineate any specific rights for the people.

A FEDERALIST VICTORY

Elected conventions in several of the smaller states quickly ratified the Constitution because it gave these states more power in the new legislative branch than they currently enjoyed under the Articles of Confederation. Other ratifying conventions didn't end so quickly or peacefully. Riots broke out in several cities throughout the United States in 1787, and public debates between Federalists and Anti-Federalists became heated. By the summer of 1788, nine of the states had ratified the Constitution, thus making it the supreme law of the land according to the ratification rules. Legislators in the four remaining states—New York, Virginia, North Carolina, and Rhode Island—hated the new Constitution but knew that they couldn't survive without the other nine.

The Federalist Papers

Debate continued to rage in the Anti-Federalist stronghold of New York. To support the Constitution, Alexander Hamilton, James Madison, and **John Jay** published a series of anonymous essays now known as *The Federalist Papers*. Written as propaganda, these essays extolled the benefits of a strong central government and allayed fears about any loss of civil liberties. Historians and political scientists now regard the essays, well written and extremely persuasive, as some of the finest writings on the Constitution and republicanism.

The Bill of Rights

Anti-Federalists in New York finally agreed to ratify the Constitution as long as the new Congress would amend the Constitution to outline specific rights and liberties reserved for the people. Madison himself wrote these ten amendments, collectively known as the **Bill of Rights**. Congress ratified the bill as the first ten amendments to the Constitution, including:

- **The First Amendment,** which protects freedom of religion, speech, and the press

- **The Second Amendment**, which guarantees the right to bear arms

- **The Fifth Amendment**, which guarantees due process of law in criminal cases

- **The Sixth Amendment**, which guarantees the right to a speedy trial by an impartial jury

- **The Ninth Amendment**, which stipulates that the people have other rights besides those specifically mentioned in the Constitution or Bill of Rights

- **The Tenth Amendment**, which awards all powers not specifically given to Congress to the individual states

Washington's Presidency

Voters in the Electoral College unanimously elected George Washington the first president in 1789 and made John Adams the vice president. Washington proved a firm, dignified, and conscientious leader. He felt his responsibility acutely, tried to remain within his branch of power, and never interfered with Congress. Washington created the first presidential cabinet to advise him. He named Alexander Hamilton secretary of the treasury, Thomas Jefferson secretary of state, and Henry Knox secretary of war.

CREATING THE JUDICIARY

Even before ratifying Madison's Bill of Rights, Congress had to create the judiciary branch of government as stipulated in the Constitution. To do so, congress passed the **Judiciary Act of 1789**, establishing a federal court system with thirteen district courts, three circuit courts, and a Supreme Court presided over by six justices. Congress, however, did not want the federal court system to have too much power over local communities and therefore designated that federal courts would primarily serve as appeals courts for cases already tried in state courts.

HAMILTON AND THE ECONOMY

Hamilton hoped to use his position as secretary of the treasury to stabilize the economy and establish a solid credit. His sound fiscal policies enabled him to achieve these goals and strengthen the national government at the expense of the individual states.

Establishing Public Credit

Hamilton knew that the United States needed capital to develop economically and to convince the rest of the world that the new government would honor debts incurred during the Revolution and under the Articles of Confederation. By 1789, the United States owed roughly $51 million, and Hamilton argued that the government should pay back the entire sum as soon as possible. He also wanted the central government to assume all the states' debts and repay creditors "at par," or with interest.

Hamilton believed that the new government should sell bonds to encourage investment from citizens and foreign interests. Congress initially fought **assumption** and **funding-at-par** but eventually conceded. These policies gave the United States a sound credit rating, allowed foreign capital to flow into the country, and stabilized the economy.

Alexander Hamilton thought a sizeable national debt would become a "national blessing," reasoning that federal debts would prevent states from drifting from the central government.

The Excise Tax

In order to raise money to pay off these debts, Hamilton suggested Congress levy an **excise tax** on liquor. Because farmers often converted their grain harvests into alcohol before shipping to save cost, many of the congressmen from agrarian states in the South and West opposed the plan and denounced it as an attempt to make northern investors richer. Congress eventually compromised and agreed to assume all federal and state debts and levy an excise tax in exchange for making the southern city of Washington, D.C., the nation's capital.

The National Bank

Next, Hamilton proposed to create a privately funded **Bank of the United States** to safely store government funds and tie wealthy Americans' interests to the stability of the federal government. Although the Constitution said nothing about creating a national bank, Hamilton argued that the document's **"elastic clause"** allowed the government to pass all laws "which shall be necessary and proper." Moreover, as a **"loose constructionist,"** he generally believed that the Constitution permitted everything it did not expressly forbid. Washington agreed and authorized creation of the bank.

Hamilton's Economic Vision

Hamilton went on to create a broad economic plan, which was primarily designed to encourage industrial growth. He asked congress to issue protective tariffs on foreign goods, subsidies, and bestow awards to encourage the formation of new businesses. Hamilton's goal was to change an essentially agricultural country into a nation with a self-sufficient industrial economy.

JEFFERSONIAN OPPOSITION

Secretary of State Thomas Jefferson opposed nearly every measure Hamilton proposed. As a **"strict constructionist,"** Jefferson believed that the Constitution forbade everything it didn't expressly permit. He therefore vehemently opposed the formation of a Bank of the United States, particularly since it seemed to benefit only the wealthy in the Northeast. He also argued against the excise tax because it unfairly punished southern and western farmers.

The Birth of Political Parties

Hamilton and Jefferson had diametrically opposed visions for the United States. Whereas Hamilton wanted a diversified industrial economy, Jefferson wanted a self-sufficient, agricultural nation. Jefferson in particular despised the thought of large cities and instead wanted a republic consisting of small farmers. These philosophical debates between Hamilton and Jefferson, com-bined with their own personal animosity for each other, split Washington's cabinet and even Congress during Washington's presidency. Eventually, two distinct political parties emerged from the feud: Hamiltonian **Federalists** and Jeffersonian **Democratic-Republicans**.

Federalists	Democratic-Republicans
Led by Adams, Hamilton, and Marshall	Led by Jefferson and Madison
Associated with aristocracy	Associated with the masses
Encouraged the development of industry	Encouraged the development of agriculture
Favored an alliance with Great Britain	Favored an alliance with France
Championed a strong central government at the expense of individual states	Championed a weak central government in favor of strengthening the states

THE INDIAN INTERCOURSE ACT

Congress passed the **Indian Intercourse Act** in 1790. The Inter-course Act stipulated that Congress would regulate all trade with Native Americans and that the United States would only acquire new western lands via official treaties. Not surprisingly, most American farmers ignored this bill and continued to steal Indian lands in the Ohio Valley. Native Americans naturally fought back in several particularly bloody skirmishes on the frontier. The fighting ended only after American forces routed the most powerful tribes at the **Battle of Fallen Timbers** in 1794.

THE WHISKEY REBELLION

A small band of Pennsylvania farmers marched toward the national capital in Philadelphia to protest Hamilton's injurious excise tax, causing rumors of another revolution to spread throughout the countryside. In response, Washington organized an army of 13,000 and marched to western Pennsylvania to end the so-called **Whiskey Rebellion** before it grew. The farmers quickly disbanded in awe of the massive display of federal force.

Washington knew it was important to show the American people that while they may have gained their independence by revolting against the crown, they could not simply revolt against any government when the mood struck them. Washington's willingness to send such an enormous force after merely hearing rumors of rebellion demonstrated the resolve of the new federal government.

THE FRENCH REVOLUTION

Washington also had many foreign crises to address, most notably the **French Revolution**. In 1789, the French overthrew King Louis XVI to the exultation of Americans. Thomas Jefferson and his supporters in particular believed that a firm friendship with a republican France would only benefit both peoples. When the revolution turned bloody, however, and war erupted between France and Great Britain, American support for France waned.

Many of the Jeffersonian Democratic-Republicans continued to back the French and believed that the United States should honor the 1778 Franco-American alliance. More conservative Americans, such as Hamilton and the Federalists, believed that the United States should ally itself with Britain.

Neutrality and Citizen Genêt

Washington finally ended the debate when he issued his **Neutrality Proclamation of 1793**, which pledged mutual friendship and the desire to trade with both nations. France's ambassador Genêt, however, ignored Washington's proclamation and continued to pursue an alliance anyway. The **Citizen Genêt Affair** outraged Federalists and Democratic-Republicans alike because it illustrated France's blatant disregard for Washington. Jefferson, though also displeased and embarrassed, eventually resigned his cabinet post for having initially supported the ambassador.

JAY'S AND PINCKNEY'S TREATIES

To prevent another war with Britain, Washington also dispatched Supreme Court Chief Justice John Jay to London in 1794 to negotiate a settlement concerning British troops still stationed on American soil. Britain eventually agreed to withdraw its troops from the Ohio Valley and pay damages for American ships the Royal Navy had illegally seized in the year after the Revolutionary War. In exchange, the United States agreed to pay outstanding pre-Revolutionary War debts to British creditors. **Jay's Treaty** angered many Democratic-Republicans who viewed the agreement as a solid first step toward a new Anglo-American alliance, which they opposed. A year later in 1795, Washington's diplomats also ended border disputes with Spain. Known as **Pinckney's Treaty**, the agreement gave Americans access to the Mississippi in exchange for promises of nonaggression in the West.

WASHINGTON'S FAREWELL

Tired of the demands of the presidency, Washington refused to run for a third term, and in 1796 he read his **Farewell Address** to the nation. In the speech, he urged Americans not to become embroiled in European affairs, and, in response to the growing political battles between Jefferson and Hamilton, warned against the dangers of factional political parties, which could ruin a nation.

> *Vermont, Tennessee, and Kentucky all joined the Union during Washington's presidency. When Washington left office, there were sixteen states in the Union.*

Adams and the Federalists

By the end of George Washington's second term, the ideological and personal differences between Thomas Jefferson and Alexander Hamilton had expanded beyond the cabinet to divide politicians throughout the country. By 1796, these two factions had coalesced into two distinct political parties. Unfortunately, neither party realized that both had the best interests of the country at heart. Debates quite often became heated and even violent as the two parties battled for control of the government.

THE ELECTION OF 1796

Two strong candidates emerged in the months prior to the election of 1796:

- Vice President John Adams for the Federalists
- Former secretary of state Thomas Jefferson for the Democratic-Republicans

Adams won the most electoral votes and thus became president, while runner-up Thomas Jefferson became vice president. The presence of a Democratic-Republican in the upper echelons of the Adams administration made it difficult at times for the new president to promote his strongly Federalist agenda.

> *Before the passage of the Twelfth Amendment in 1804, the Constitution stipulated that the presidential candidate who received the second highest number of electoral votes would become vice president.*

UNDECLARED WARFARE WITH FRANCE

The first test of Adams's mettle came from France in 1796, when Paris ended all diplomatic relations with the United States in response to improved Anglo-American relations outlined in Jay's Treaty with Britain. Washington's Neutrality Proclamation and Jay's Treaty had both stunned France, which had expected the United States to honor the Franco–American alliance made during the Revolutionary War. Consequently, French warships began seizing hundreds of American merchant ships and millions of dollars' worth of cargo without cause or compensation.

The XYZ Affair

Hoping to avoid war with France, Adams sent ambassadors to Paris to normalize relations in 1797. When the emissaries arrived, however, the French officials, nicknamed by the American press X, Y, and Z, demanded a bribe of a quarter of a million dollars before they would even speak with the Americans. The **XYZ Affair** outraged Congress and the American public, and prompted many to cry, "Millions for defense, but not one cent for tribute!" Adams's popularity skyrocketed when he refused the request and prepared for war. Although Congress never officially declared war with France, both countries waged undeclared naval warfare in the Atlantic for several years.

The war ended shortly before Adams left office, when he signed the **Convention of 1800,** in which he promised U.S. merchants would not seek payment for seized cargo in exchange for the annulment of the Franco–American alliance.

THE ALIEN AND SEDITION ACTS

Adams's sudden boost in popularity in the wake of the XYZ Affair gave Federalists in Congress the confidence to boldly strengthen the federal government. In 1798, Congress passed the **Alien and Sedition Acts** in part to prevent French revolutionaries from entering the United States but also to cripple the Democratic-Republicans:

- **The Alien Act** extended the time required for foreigners to become American citizens from five years to fourteen years and gave Congress the power to expel aliens. This act was aimed directly at Irish and French immigrants, who mainly supported the Democratic-Republicans.

- **The Sedition Act** banned public criticism of the president and Congress and was used to silence Democratic-Republican newspapers.

The Virginia and Kentucky Resolutions

Instead of weakening the Democratic-Republicans, the Alien and Sedition Acts only made them stronger. For the first time, Jeffersonians organized as a true opposition party in Congress: they formed caucuses, selected party leaders, and promoted a platform. They also challenged Federalists for the previously nonpartisan position of Speaker of the House.

Democratic-Republicans throughout the country vehemently protested the Sedition Act as a violation of their First Amendment right to free speech. Vice President Jefferson and James Madison even anonymously drafted the **Virginia and Kentucky Resolutions** later that year, in which they proclaimed the Alien and Sedition Acts null and void in those states. The resolutions argued that because the states had formed a compact in creating the Union, the states therefore reserved the right to nullify any congressional laws they deemed unconstitutional.

Jefferson and Madison's Virginia and Kentucky Resolutions were two of the most influential American works written before the Civil War. Arguing that member states had the authority to nullify unconstitutional acts of Congress, the resolutions effectively claimed the power of judicial review for the states, not the Supreme Court. The resolutions also sparked the first debate over whether the states or the federal government had the final authority. Future Democrats—the political descendents of the Democratic-Republicans—would continue this line of reasoning.

Did the Federalists or the Democratic-Republicans have a more profound effect on the formation of the United States?

Even though Democratic-Republican presidents dominated the White House during twenty-four of the first thirty-six years of the Early Republic, the Federalists had the greatest overall effect on the actual formation of the United States. To start, the Federalists were the primary force behind the ratification of the U.S. Constitution. In addition, the Federalists created a federal tax system and a national bank, which provided a stable economy. Finally, by strengthening the Supreme Court and more clearly defining the relationship between federal and state law, the Federalists greatly influenced the federal legal system. All of these factors contributed to the more stable and unified country we enjoy today.

The Federalists used their influence throughout the fall of 1787 and the winter and spring of 1788 to persuade the states to unanimously ratify the Constitution and establish the multibranched structure of the U.S. government. Patriots and Anti-Federalists like Patrick Henry and Samuel Adams opposed ratification. They believed that the newly structured federal government would be too powerful and constricting and that Congress should not have the right to tax all Americans. Most important, Anti-Federalists feared the new office of the presidency would be a modified form of monarchy. The Patriots and Anti-Federalists also believed that republicanism would never survive in a large country, because the government would be too distant from the hearts and minds of the people they represented. In *The Federalist Papers*, Alexander Hamilton, John Jay, and James Madison argued that republicanism would work well for the United States. In fact, because the republic would be so large with so many conflicting constituencies, no single faction would ever be able to dominate the others. Additional safeguards in the Constitution, such as the separation of powers and the system of checks and balances, would further prevent the government from ever becoming too powerful. Federalist arguments such as these helped generate the support necessary to ratify the Constitution.

Student Essay

The economic policies of another Federalist, Secretary of the Treasury Alexander Hamilton, further contributed to the structure of the federal government and helped put the nation on a sound financial footing. Despite protests from Thomas Jefferson and the Democratic-Republicans, Hamilton urged President Washington and Congress to support the development of American manufacturing, pass the Excise Tax to fund the government, assume all state and federal debts, fund those debts at par, and to create a Central Bank of the United States. Even though the Constitution didn't specifically authorize any of these measures, Hamilton and the Federalists insisted the Constitution permitted everything that it did not expressly forbid. Democratic-Republicans were outraged; as "strict constructionists," they believed that the Constitution forbade everything it did not expressly allow. Clearly, the United States was fortunate to have strong Federalist supporters. Assumption and funding at par gave the country credibility and encouraged speculators to invest in American enterprises. The Excise Tax filled the federal treasury, and the Bank of the United States helped stabilize the economy.

Finally, it was the Federalists under Chief Justice John Marshall who gave the United States its legal infrastructure. Most of Marshall's rulings during his thirty-five years as Chief Justice bolstered the federal government against the individual states. In *Marbury v. Madison*, for example, he secured the power of judicial review for the Supreme Court. In subsequent cases, Marshall would also defend the Court's superior position to state courts. In doing so, Marshall legitimized the federal government and set strong legal precedents for the relationship between federal and state courts.

Without the Federalists, the United States would look vastly different than it does today. Specifically, the Federalists gave the country a flexible Constitution, a structured economic system, and a legal system with the power to review actions taken by the other branches of government. Most important, all these actions led to the concept of a single nation, instead of a loose commonwealth of states that acted more like independent countries.

Test Questions and Answers

1. Why did most Americans in the 1770s want the type of government created under the Articles of Confederation?

- Americans didn't want a strong central government or ruler after defeating the tyrant King George III.

- Most wanted independent, small republics to better represent the interests of the people.

2. What were the different strengths of the Articles of Confederation and the Constitution?

- The Articles made concessions for local representation, locally collected taxes, and gave the bulk of the power to the states.

- The Constitution centralized power, increased the economic strength of the nation, and created a more cohesive country.

3. What was the Whiskey Rebellion, and what was its historical significance?

- Local farmers rebelled against what they considered to be an unfair tax in the distillation of whiskey.

- Suppressing the rebellion became a test of strength and will for the new federal government.

- The federal government proved it was willing to use military force to maintain its power over the states.

4. What was Madison's role in creating the Constitution?

- Madison has become known as the "Father of the Constitution."

- He strengthened the government by organizing executive, congressional, and judicial branches.

- He wrote the *Federalist Papers* in support of federalism and the Constitution.

- He wrote the Bill of Rights.

Timeline

1781	The Second Continental Congress ratifies the Articles of Confederation.
1785	Congress passes the Land Ordinance of 1785.
1786	Shays's Rebellion occurs.
	Protesters attack courthouses in Massachusetts.
	Delegates meet to discuss revising Articles of Confederation in Annapolis, Maryland.
1787	Congress passes the Northwest Ordinance of 1787.
	The Constitutional Convention is held in Philadelphia, Pennsylvania.
	Alexander Hamilton, John Jay, and James Madison begin writing the *Federalist Papers*.
1788	Nine states ratify the new Constitution.
1789	George Washington becomes the first president.
	Congress passes the Judiciary Act of 1789.
1790	Congress passes the Indian Intercourse Act.
1791	The Bill of Rights is ratified.
	The Bank of the United States is created.
	Congress levies an excise tax.
1792	Washington is reelected.
1793	Washington issues the Neutrality Proclamation.
	The Citizen Genêt affair outrages the American public.
1794	A band of farmers march the capital to protest the excise tax in the Whiskey Rebellion.
	Fighting between Native Americans and American farmers finally ends in the Battle of Fallen Timbers.
	Jay's Treaty angers Democratic-Republicans who oppose an Anglo-American alliance.
1795	Pinckney's Treaty gives Americans access to the Mississippi.
1796	Washington reads his Farewell Address.
	John Adams is elected president.

1797	French officials demand a bribe in the XYZ Affair.
1798	Congress passes the Alien and Sedition Acts.
	U.S. wages undeclared naval war with France.
	Jefferson and Madison write the Virginia and Kentucky Resolutions.

Major Figures

John Adams A prominent Bostonian lawyer, Adams first became famous for defending the British soldiers accused of murdering five civilians in the Boston Massacre. He was a delegate from Massachusetts in the Continental Congresses, where he rejected proposals for home rule. He served as vice president to George Washington and was president of the United States from 1797–1801.

Alexander Hamilton A brilliant New York lawyer and statesman, Hamilton at thirty-two years old was one of the youngest framers of the Constitution at the Constitutional Convention in 1787. An ardent Federalist, he supported the Constitution during the ratification debates even though he actually believed that the new document was still too weak. He helped write the *Federalist Papers*, which are now regarded as some of the finest essays on American government and republicanism. He served as the first Secretary of the Treasury under President George Washington and is responsible for establishing the first Bank of the United States and the national credit.

John Jay Coauthor of *The Federalist Papers*, Jay worked tirelessly to convince Anti-federalist New Yorkers to ratify the Constitution. He served as the first Chief Justice of the Supreme Court and became one of the most hated men in America after he negotiated Jay's Treaty in 1794 with Great Britain.

Thomas Jefferson A Virginian planter and lawyer, Jefferson played an invaluable role in the revolutionary cause when he drafted the Declaration of Independence in 1776, justifying American independence from Great Britain. He later served as the first secretary of state under President George Washington and as vice president to John Adams. He was elected president in 1800 and 1804.

James Madison Originally a Federalist, Madison supported the ratification of the Constitution to replace the Articles of Confederation, and wrote some of the best essays on American government and republicanism as coauthor of the *Federalist Papers*. He also personally drafted the Bill of Rights, afraid that the Constitution might be amended if handed to a committee. After ratification, he began supporting southern and western agrarian interests as a Democratic-Republican. While in retirement in Virginia, Madison coauthored the Virginia and Kentucky Resolutions with Thomas Jefferson in 1798. He later reentered politics and was eventually elected president in

1808 and again in 1812. As the fourth president, Madison promoted the development of southern and western agriculture as his predecessor and friend Thomas Jefferson had. He repealed the Embargo Act, but supported the Non–Intercourse Act and Macon's Bill No. 2. He led the United States in the War of 1812.

Daniel Shays A depressed western Massachusetts farmer, Shays led approximately 1,500 fellow farmers in a revolt against the state legislature in Boston in 1786. State officials easily ended Shays's Rebellion and pardoned all but two of the would-be revolutionaries. Shays escaped to Vermont and finally settled in New York. His revolt was only one of many launched against state governments in the mid-1780s, and prompted prominent Americans to discuss amending the Articles of Confederation.

George Washington A young Virginian planter and militia officer, Washington began the French and Indian War in 1754. He later became commander in chief of the American forces during the Revolutionary War and first president of the United States in 1789. Although he lost most of the battles he fought, his leadership skills were unparalleled and were integral to the creation of the United States.

Suggested Reading

- Ellis, Joseph. *Founding Brothers: The Revolutionary Generation.* New York: Vintage, 2000.

This Pulitzer Prize–winning book discusses the shaping of the United States immediately after the revolution, focussing on pivotal interactions between George Washington, Benjamin Franklin, Alexander Hamilton, Thomas Jefferson, John Adams, James Madison, and Aaron Burr. Ellis vividly illustrates the high-stakes of post-revolutionary politics.

- Ellis, Joseph. *His Excellency: George Washington.* New York: Knopf, 2004.

The latest of many biographies of George Washington, *His Excellency* comes from the author of several previous books on men of the Revolutionary era, including *Founding Brothers.* Ellis tries to strip away most of the myth that has been built up around Washington, and to portray him as he was received in his day.

- Hamilton, Alexander, James Madison, and John Jay. *The Federalist Papers.* Supplementary materials written by Maria Hong. New York: Pocket Books, 2004.

The eighty-five essays that compose the *Federalist Papers* have become the foundation for our interpretation of the U.S. Constitution. Amazingly, they were written very hastily by three men—John Jay, James Madison, and Alexander Hamilton—in an effort to persuade the public and delegates to the Constitutional Convention of 1787 to ratify the new U.S. Constitution. They are forceful, brilliant pieces and required reading for anyone interested in the intricacies of the U.S. government.

- McCullough, David. *John Adams.* New York: Simon & Schuster, 2002.

This award-winning biography of John Adams is meticulously researched and based largely on Adams's numerous personal journals and letters to his wife.

Republican Agrarianism: 1800–1824

- The Election of 1800
- Republicans in Power
- The War of 1812
- The Era of Good Feelings

Many historians argue that the election of 1800 had as much impact on American and world history as the Declaration of Independence and the Revolutionary War because it proved democracy worked. With the election, or "revolution," in 1800, the Federalist party lost the White House to the Democratic-Republicans. This transfer of power without bloodshed was a remarkable feat at the time, and one that brought Thomas Jefferson to the presidency.

Although Jefferson had planned to decrease the size and influence of the federal government and return power to state legislatures, he ironically strengthened the government by bending the Constitution to purchase land. Moreover, his plans to punish Britain and France for unprovoked naval attacks floundered, and his foreign policy ultimately caused a nationwide depression. Britain and the United States eventually fought another war over sovereignty issues that finally ended in a stalemate two years later. Still, Americans emerged from the war with a newfound sense of national pride and unity that helped them focus on improving national infrastructure in the early nineteenth century.

The Election of 1800

As the presidential election of 1800 approached, problems mounted for President Adams and the Federalists. The Alien and Sedition Acts, Jay's Treaty, and the suppression of the Whiskey Rebellion by federal troops had all soured Americans' opinion of the Federalists. Still, Federalists nominated both **John Adams** and Charles C. Pinckney, while Democratic-Republicans selected **Thomas Jefferson** and Aaron Burr to run for president.

JEFFERSON ELECTED

Although Adams received a significant number of electoral votes, he still won fewer than both Jefferson and Burr. Both Democratic-Republican candidates, had tied with seventy-three votes each, thus forcing the House of Representatives to determine the next president. Most Federalists lobbied representatives to elect Burr, but Alexander Hamilton succeeded in convincing his colleagues to vote for his arch-nemesis Jefferson because he hated Burr even more. As a result, Jefferson became the nation's third president and Burr his vice president.

> Until 1804, the presidential candidate who received the most votes became president, and the second-place candidate was vice president, even if they represented different parties. The **Twelfth Amendment** to the Constitution stipulated that candidates for the respective positions would run together on the same party ticket instead of against each other for the presidency. Congress ratified the amendment to avoid a tie in the Electoral College similar to that in the election of 1800.

THE REVOLUTION OF 1800

Historians often refer to the election of 1800 as the **Revolution of 1800** because the Federalists ceded power to the Democratic-Republicans entirely without violence, a truly significant accomplishment given the fact that so many wars in Europe had begun when one party had refused to relinquish control to another. For this reason, the Revolution of 1800 was just as momentous as the Revolution of 1776. Whereas the American Revolution had established the United States as an independent nation, the election of 1800 proved that the new nation would survive.

> The election also proved, contrary to George Washington's belief, that political parties would not rip apart the republic. Rather, they actually served as a vehicle for peaceful discussion and exchange without bloodshed.

Adams's Midnight Judges

Shortly before they transferred power to the Democratic-Republicans, Federalists in congress passed the **Judiciary Act of 1801** to ensure that Federalists would continue to control the courts during Jefferson's presidency. Adams even used his last remaining hours as president to appoint a new chief justice to the Supreme Court and forty-two other **"midnight judges"** to lower federal courts.

Republicans in Power

Jefferson came to power promising to reduce the size of the federal government and deemphasize industry in favor of agriculture. Jefferson argued that these actions would set the United States back on its "rightful" course toward agrarian republicanism and redefine the role of the government so it would be less intrusive in the lives of American citizens. He slashed federal spending, virtually disbanded the army and navy, and repealed almost all taxes except those on the sale of federal lands. By selling public lands, Jefferson hoped to encourage the creation of more small farms and rid the government of debt.

MARBURY V. MADISON

Soon after taking office, the Democratic-Republicans proceeded to repeal the bulk of Federalist legislation, including the Alien and Sedition Acts and the Judiciary Act of 1801. Jefferson and his secretary of state, **James Madison,** also refused to honor the appointments of Adams's "midnight judges." Outraged, one Federalist justice named William Marbury sued Madison, and in 1803 the Supreme Court heard the case. Chief Justice **John Marshall** sympathized with fellow Federalist Marbury but ruled in the landmark decision *Marbury v. Madison* that even though the president should have honored Adams's appointments, the Supreme Court had no power over Jefferson in this matter because the Judiciary Act of 1789 was unconstitutional. This decision allowed Marshall to simultaneously give Jefferson his victory and strengthen the Supreme Court with the power of **judicial review**, or the right to declare laws passed by Congress unconstitutional.

THE LOUISIANA PURCHASE

Jefferson overstepped his authority as president again in 1803 when he purchased the vast tract of land between the Mississippi River and the Rocky Mountains from Napoleon in France. Although Jefferson knew the Constitution didn't authorize presidents to purchase land, he also realized he had to act on the unprecedented opportunity to double the size of the country for only 15 million dollars. The **Louisiana Purchase** gave Americans control of most of the Mississippi River and ended French dreams of a North American empire.

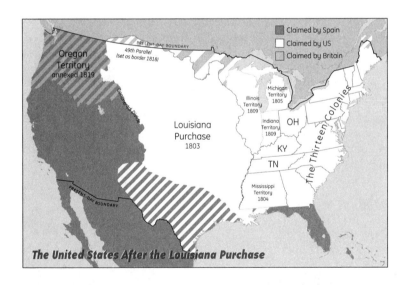

The United States After the Louisiana Purchase

Ironically, Jefferson, a Democratic-Republican who despised taxes, purchased the Louisiana Territory with money earned from Federalist taxes collected during Washington and Adams's presidencies. However, Napoleon had just offered him more land than he had ever hoped to be able to purchase from France. How could he refuse?

LEWIS AND CLARK

In 1803, Jefferson asked Congress to fund an exploratory expedition to the Pacific Northwest, ostensibly "for the purpose of extending the foreign commerce of the United States" mainly by finding a water route to the Pacific Ocean. Jefferson also wanted to map the unexplored Louisiana Territory and foster trade relations with the indigenous Native Americans. With Congress's approval, Jefferson assigned his secretary Meriwether Lewis and army captain William Clark to lead the **"Corps of Discovery"** expedition.

Lewis and Clark embarked on their journey from St. Louis with approximately fifty men in 1804 and returned more than two years later in 1806. They found no easy water route to the Pacific, but returned with maps and information about the terrain, people, and natural resources that would fuel the pioneering spirit of countless Americans.

EMBARGO ACT

France sold the Louisiana Territory to Jefferson primarily because Napoleon needed money to fund his war with Great Britain as he continued to try to conquer the whole of Europe. Although far removed from the fighting, the war nevertheless hurt American trade across the Atlantic. Both the French and English navies frequently seized American ships looking for arms, supplies, and other contraband even though the United States had declared neutrality. Unable to convince either side to respect American neutral shipping rights, Congress and Jefferson decided that American merchants would simply not trade with Europe any more, and passed the **Embargo Act** in 1807, prohibiting trade with the United States. Democratic-Republicans hoped that the embargo would cripple both France and England and force them to respect American shipping rights.

Impressment

Britain complicated the situation by forcing American sailors from seized ships into military service on British warships. Although Royal Navy officials claimed they only impressed their own deserters, records have shown that British officers illegally impressed more than 5,000 American men. Americans at home viewed Britain's policy of **impressment** as an affront to their hard-won liberties and as a violation of the Treaty of Paris that had ended the Revolutionary War.

In what was to become known as the **Chesapeake Affair**, war fever raged once again in the United States when on June 22, 1802, a British ship attacked a U.S. warship, the *Chesapeake*, and then impressed four American sailors. Jefferson wanted to avoid war, but also knew that he couldn't simply ignore Britain's blatant violations of American sovereignty. Congress passed Jefferson's Embargo Acto of 1807 on December 22, six months to the day after the British attacked the *Chesapeake*.

The Embargo's Impact

The Embargo Act crippled the American economy far more than it hurt Britain or France, as American exports fell from $109 million to $22 million in the first year alone. Depression followed soon after, when farmers in the West and South couldn't sell any grain, cotton, or tobacco to the lucrative markets abroad. Rumblings of secession even spread throughout the hardest-hit areas in the northern states. Still, Jefferson refused to lift the embargo, and it remained in effect until Congress finally repealed it in 1809.

ELECTION OF 1808

The depression caused by Thomas Jefferson's Embargo Act weakened the Democratic-Republican Party in the 1808 national elections. Although **James Madison** still managed to defeat the Federalist candidate Charles Pinckney for the presidency, the party lost seats in Congress. As Jefferson's chosen successor,

Madison carried out his fellow Virginian's policies throughout both of his presidential terms.

TECUMSEH AND THE PROPHET

One of Madison's greatest challenges during his first term involved the growing Native American threat to American settlers in the West. American farmers had eagerly pushed westward into the Mississippi River basin since Jefferson's Louisiana Purchase, despite Congress's promise to respect Native American territory in the Indian Intercourse Act of 1790. Frustrated, two Shawnee brothers named **Tecumseh** and Tenskwatawa, nicknamed the Prophet for reportedly having a series of "visions," succeeded in creating a pan-Indian alliance called the **Northwest Confederacy** (including the Shawnee, Cherokee, Choctaw, Chickasaws, and Creeks, among other tribes), which sought a return to traditional ways of Native American life. Fearing another Native American uprising, Madison ordered Indiana Territory Governor **William Henry Harrison** to destroy the Confederacy, which he did in 1811 at the **Battle of Tippecanoe**.

> *Harrison's success at the Battle of Tippecanoe made him famous throughout the United States. He would later capitalize on his fame by running for the presidency in 1836 and 1840, using the rallying cry "Tippecanoe and Tyler, too!" Tyler was Harrison's running mate in the election.*

CHAPTER 5
1800–1824

The War of 1812

By 1810, many of the older and experienced statesmen in Congress had retired, leaving their seats open to a young and passionate new generation. Most of these young congressmen came from the southern and western states and yearned for action. These **"War Hawks,"** like **John C. Calhoun** and **Henry Clay,** had ordered Harrison to defeat Tecumseh and the Prophet and clamored for a new war against Great Britain. Although President Madison hoped to avoid war, he eventually caved to pressures from the War Hawks and requested that Congress declare war against Britain in June of 1812.

NON-INTERCOURSE ACT AND MACON'S BILL NUMBER 2

Because the Embargo Act had failed, Congress passed the **Non-Intercourse Act** in 1809 to reopen trade with every country *except* France and Britain. When this too failed, Congress then passed **Macon's Bill Number 2** in 1810 to entice Britain and France into recognizing American shipping rights. The bill stipulated that the United States would reward the first of the two to respect American shipping by reinstating the embargo on the country that did not.

Hoping to bring the Americans into the war, Napoleon ordered French ships to respect American merchants, thus forcing Madison to reinstate the embargo on trade with Britain. After two more years of British aggression on the Atlantic and in the West, Madison eventually had no choice but to heed War Hawk demands and ask Congress to declare war on Britain.

CAUSES OF THE WAR OF 1812

Americans clamored for war with Britain in 1812 for two reasons: to defeat the British-backed Native Americans in the Ohio Valley and to defend American shipping rights and end the practice of impressments. Despite these goals, many Americans in the West also wanted war in order to seize more land, particularly in British Canada.

A STALEMATED WAR

The war itself went badly for the United States. Thanks to Jefferson's belief in frugal government, the U.S. Navy consisted of just a few ineffective gunboats, and the army had very few men, weapons, or supplies. American forces had some success in the Northwest but couldn't manage to punch through the British blockade of the eastern ports or prevent the burning of Washington, D.C. The war, for all practical purposes, was a stalemate, and both countries signed the **Treaty of Ghent** in 1814 to end it. The treaty essentially stipulated that neither side had gained or lost any territory, and neither side mentioned impressment or the illegal seizure of American ships. Ironically, American troops under the command of General **Andrew Jackson** won a resounding victory in early January 1815 at the **Battle of New Orleans**, just days after diplomats had signed the peace treaty.

THE HARTFORD CONVENTION

While the American and British delegations negotiated the treaty in Ghent, Federalist delegates from five New England states met in Hartford, Connecticut, to discuss their dissatisfaction with "Mr. Madison's War." In fact, some felt so outraged that they proposed secession from the Union. After meeting for several weeks, delegates at the **Hartford Convention** settled on merely petitioning Congress with a list of four major grievances:

- The federal government should compensate New England shippers for profits lost during the war.

- The Constitution should be amended so that states can vote on important decisions that affect the entire Union, such as the admission of new states and declaring war.

- The executive office should be changed so that presidents can only serve one term and cannot come from the same state as the previous president.

- The Three-Fifths Clause should be stricken from the Constitution.

The Hartford Convention's list of demands reflected northern dissatisfaction with the federal government and with the war. Of the first five presidents, only one of them—John Adams—had not been a member of the so-called **Virginia Dynasty,** which consisted of Washington, Jefferson, Madison, and Monroe, all from Virginia. This strong southern representation in the White House frustrated many New Englanders, who felt that they had been left out of the political loop. This frustration was the true driving force behind the delegates' list of demands.

Unfortunately for the Hartford delegates, their petition arrived in Washington, D.C., just as news of Jackson's victory in New Orleans arrived and the Treaty of Ghent was signed. The effect on

CHAPTER 5 1800–1824

the Federalists was devastating as the country voiced its support of the war and of the government. The Federalist Party never recovered from the stigma of disloyalty.

> Although Americans today usually associate secession with the South, New Englanders at the Hartford Convention were actually the first to threaten to leave the Union. Talk of secession among states in the early part of the nineteenth century was much more common than in mid-century, though.

The Era of Good Feelings

Despite the fact that the United States had gained nothing from the War of 1812, Americans felt intensely patriotic when the conflict ended in 1814. Jackson's victory at the Battle of New Orleans made Americans particularly proud, as if they had won a "second war for independence" against the most powerful army in the world. This newfound American spirit also boosted the popularity of the War Hawks, like Clay and Calhoun, who emerged as the nation's new congressional leaders in the postwar era.

Democratic-Republican **James Monroe** easily defeated his weak Federalist opponent, Rufus King, in the election of 1816, and in doing so not only effectively killed the Federalist Party, but also ushered in an era of domestic tranquility and single-party rule. One newspaper in Boston, the *Columbian Centinel,* dubbed these virtually controversy-free years the **Era of Good Feelings**. The name stuck.

CLAY'S AMERICAN SYSTEM

As the leader of the War Hawks, Speaker of the House Henry Clay proposed a three-pronged **"American System"** to improve the national infrastructure of the United States. Clay's nationalistic system included:

- Improving the financial sector of the economy. Under his leadership, Congress created the **Second Bank of the**

United States in 1816 to offer easy credit and stabilize the economy.

- Protecting struggling American manufacturers from the postwar influx of cheap British goods. He pushed the **Tariff of 1816** through Congress to place a 20 percent tax on all foreign goods. This also happened to be the first tariff Congress passed to protect industry rather than merely to increase revenue.

- Connecting the country via a system of roads and canals built with money raised from the new protective tariff. These **internal improvements** would help farmers ship their crops and goods to the East and manufacturers to ship their products to the West.

POSTWAR EXPANSION

The Era of Good Feelings at home affected foreign policy as well. Most significantly, the United States ended decades of hostility with Great Britain with the following agreements:

- **The Rush-Bagot Agreement** in 1817 to demilitarize the Great Lakes region

- **The Treaty of 1818** to establish a clear border between the United States and Canada from Minnesota to the Rocky Mountains at the forty-ninth parallel. The treaty also specified that the United States would jointly occupy the Oregon Territory in the Pacific Northwest (present-day Oregon, Idaho, Washington, British Columbia, and part of Montana) until 1828.

New States

Settlers carved out three new territories in the Deep South after the war:

- Louisiana became a state in 1812.

- Mississippi became a state in 1817.

- Alabama became a state in 1819.

Seizing Spanish Florida

General **Andrew Jackson**, meanwhile, illegally seized Spanish Florida on the pretext that Spain had plotted with the Seminole Indian tribe against the United States. Spain ultimately ceded Florida to the United States in 1819 in exchange for Washington's retraction on claims to Spanish Texas.

THE MONROE DOCTRINE

In 1823, John Quincy Adams devised the **Monroe Doctrine**. It represented the Monroe administration's most significant foreign policy achievement. The Monroe Doctrine stipulated that:

- European powers had to stay away from the New World.

- Old World powers could keep the colonies they currently had, but could not establish any new ones.

- America would support the growth of democracy throughout the western hemisphere.

British policy-makers had originally suggested the Monroe Doctrine to Monroe and Adams because they wanted to protect their West Indian colonies from the continental powers in Europe. Secretly, the British also feared American expansionism in the Caribbean and hoped that a joint declaration against intervention in the New World would both curb European aggression and stymie American plans. Adams realized that Britain wanted to bind the United States as much as it wanted to bind the rest of Europe, and so he encouraged Monroe to issue the doctrine on his own so as not to cripple American interests.

Even though the British failed to contain the United States, they still supported the Monroe Doctrine anyway and used Royal Navy warships to enforce it. The Monroe Doctrine allowed new Latin American democracies to flourish without fear of war with Spain, France, or Portugal.

JOHN MARSHALL AND THE SUPREME COURT

The Supreme Court issued a series of rulings during the Era of Good Feelings that also increased the power of the federal gov-

The Monroe Doctrine has since become a major tenet of American foreign policy, used and sometimes abused by U.S. presidents since Monroe to intervene and occasionally control developing South and Central American countries. Theodore Roosevelt famously added his "Roosevelt Corollary" to the Monroe Doctrine at the end of the nineteenth century to limit European nations' use of force to collect debts from Latin American countries.

ernment. The Court, still dominated by diehard Federalist Chief Justice **John Marshall**, upheld federal power more out of Hamiltonian beliefs in strong government than out of love for the new nationalism. The rulings included:

- *Dartmouth College v. Woodward* that states could not nullify or amend legal contracts (1819)

- *Cohens v. Virginia* that the Supreme Court had the authority to review decisions reached in the supreme courts of the individual states (1821)

- *McCulloch v. Maryland* that neither Hamiltonian "loose" interpretations of the elastic clause nor the Bank of the United States violated the Constitution (1819)

- *Gibbons v. Ogden* that Congress had the authority to regulate interstate commerce (1824)

Marshall's rulings during these early years played a huge role in consolidating the power of the federal government over the individual states and ensured that Federalist ideals would live on despite the party's early death.

THE PANIC OF 1819

A string of crises beginning at the end of Monroe's first term quickly dampened the "good feelings" of the era. The first crisis hit in the **Panic of 1819** and was caused at least in part by a change in credit policies of the Second Bank of the United States (SBUS) toward a more conservative lending policy. The bank was concerned about the practices of the rough-and-tumble **wildcat banks** in the West that were lending money quickly and without as much concern for regulations as other banks. The SBUS called in loans made to these banks, forcing the banks to call in loans they had made to thousands of pioneers along the frontier, mainly farmers. The new policies, combined with price declines in many agricultural areas, forced thousands of farmers off their land. The number of Americans in poverty and debtor prisons swelled for almost a decade until the economy rebounded.

INCREASING SECTIONALISM

Sectional tensions also arose in 1819 when the Missouri Territory applied for admission to the Union as a new slave state. Even though Missouri had met all of the qualifications, the northern-dominated House of Representatives denied the territory state-hood because they didn't want to tip the sectional balance in the Senate in favor of the South with twelve slave states to only eleven free. The House then passed the **Tallmadge Amendment** in 1819 to gradually free slave children and declare that settlers couldn't take any more slaves into the territory.

THE MISSOURI COMPROMISE

Southern elites were outraged at what they acutely believed to be northern attempts to eliminate slavery. By 1819, they had become almost completely dependent on slave labor to produce cotton and reasoned that if slavery couldn't expand westward, then the southern way of life would certainly die. In other words, they feared that northerners in the free states would hem them in geographically and suffocate them economically. People in the South also feared that banning slavery in Missouri would set a precedent for all other new states. As a result, they rejected the Tallmadge Amendment in the Senate and then deadlocked Congress for several more months until House Speaker Henry Clay proposed the **Missouri Compromise**. Both southerners and northerners agreed to the following:

- Missouri would be admitted as a slave state.

- Maine would simultaneously be admitted as a free state to maintain the sectional balance.

- Slavery was declared illegal north of the 36° 30' parallel west of Missouri.

Impact of the Compromise

The Missouri Compromise of 1819 saved the Union from a potentially divisive issue. Most southerners liked the compromise because the slave South could expand westward. Northerners, on the other hand, also liked the compromise because slavery South of the 36° 30' parallel kept slavery contained in the South and out of most lands acquired in the vast Louisiana Purchase, which was a free territory. With the slavery issue at least temporarily settled, Americans could now focus on other matters.

*An elderly **Thomas Jefferson** wrote that the Missouri Compromise, "like a fire bell in the night awakened and filled me with terror. I considered it at once as the knell of the Union." The conflict over the expansion of slavery in new territories ultimately tore the Union apart in the Civil War.*

CHAPTER 5
1800–1824

John Marshall served as chief justice of the Supreme Court for thirty-five years, from 1801 to 1836. In what ways did his rulings help establish the power of the Supreme Court?

The rulings of Chief Justice John Marshall, who served on the Supreme Court for thirty-five years under six presidents, were pivotal in establishing the authority of the Supreme Court. Marshall's belief in the supremacy of the federal government and of the Supreme Court over the power of individual states is illustrated in three early court cases: *Marbury v. Madison*, *Dartmouth College v. Woodward*, and *McCulloch v. Maryland*. Marshall's rulings in each of these cases helped to establish the authority of the Supreme Court.

Marbury v. Madison in 1803 helped establish the Supreme Court's authority in interpreting the U.S. Constitution. On his last day in office, President Adams had appointed William Marbury to serve as justice of the peace for the District of Columbia. However, Adams failed to submit the commission before midnight. James Madison, the secretary of state under the new administration, refused to accept Marbury's commission. Marbury petitioned the Supreme Court for a writ of mandamus that would force Madison to honor his commission. Marshall did not rule in favor of Marbury, despite the fact that he himself had been appointed by Adams the day before Marbury had been appointed. Instead, Marshall boldly declared that the Supreme Court did not have the authority to issue a writ of mandamus. By doing so, Marshall ruled that sections of the Judiciary Act of 1789, which created the Supreme Court and were the basis of Marbury's petition, were unconstitutional. Marshall's ruling became monumental because it set the precedent of judicial review, wherein the Supreme Court could declare a congressional act unconstitutional.

Sixteen years later in 1819, Marshall issued another defining decision in the case of *Dartmouth College v. Woodward*. Controversy first arose when New Hampshire's legislature attempted to transform Dartmouth College into a public institution because it wanted to replace Dartmouth's Federalist-dominated Board of Trustees with a state-created Republican governing board. Marshall sided in favor of Dartmouth on the grounds that

Student Essay

Dartmouth's founding charter of 1769, issued by the King of England, was essentially a contract, and the Constitution prohibited state governments from interfering with contracts. Marshall's ruling severely limited the regulatory power of the state government, once more affirming his Federalist conviction of federal power over the power of the states.

McCulloch v. Maryland, also in 1819, was an even more monumental case dealing with the boundaries of state government. In 1816, President Madison reintroduced the Bank of the United States, which, in turn, established a local branch in Baltimore. Maryland maintained its right to tax the bank, which outraged the bank's cashier, James McCulloch, who refused to pay. The first question considered by the Court was whether Congress had the authority to charter a national bank. Using a loose interpretation of the Constitution, Marshall decided that it did. The next question was whether a state could tax an agency of the federal government. Marshall eventually overruled Maryland on the grounds that states did not have such authority. He maintained that constitutional law was more fundamental than individual state laws since it was created to govern all the states collectively. His ruling angered Republicans but left no doubt about the court's position: states were subordinate to the federal government.

Marshall's presence on the Supreme Court for more than three decades significantly shaped the power of the Court and of the federal government during their formative years. In *Marbury v. Madison*, Marshall set a precedent for the Supreme Court's power to determine whether or not a law or act is constitutional. In the two cases, *Dartmouth College v. Woodward* and *McCulloch v. Maryland*, Marshall's rulings helped establish the boundaries for state government. Marshall's bold decisions validated the very authority of the Supreme Court. Moreover, his interpretations of the Constitution upheld that document's authority as the foundation of law in the United States.

Test Questions and Answers

1. Why is the election of 1800 often referred to as the Revolution of 1800?

- It marked the transfer of power from the Federalists to the Republicans.

- It marked the first peaceful transfer of power between two bitter political rivals and thus proved that democracy could work.

2. What were the causes of the War of 1812?

- Americans in the East wanted to protect their shipping rights as a neutral nation.

- Americans in the West wanted to win more territory in the North and West.

3. What court cases helped pave the way for continued economic growth in 1819?

- *Dartmouth College v. Woodward* secured the viability of contracts and determined that states could not interfere with legal contracts.

- *McCulloch v. Maryland* checked the power of the state governments and strengthened the central government in matters of finances.

- *Gibbons v. Ogden* established federal supremacy in regulating interstate commerce.

4. How was foreign policy expressed through the Monroe Doctrine?

- The doctrine established the concept of "spheres of influence."

- The doctrine declared that the United States had influence over the Western hemisphere.

- The doctrine claimed that fundamental differences existed between American and European systems and that any

European attempt to settle in the Americas would be considered dangerous to the United States and its people.

- The doctrine told European powers not to establish any new colonies in the New World.

CHAPTER 5
1800-1824

Timeline

1800	The Convention of 1800 ends the war with France.
	Thomas Jefferson is elected president of the United States.
1801	Congress passes the Judiciary Act of 1801.
1802	Congress repeals the Judiciary Act of 1801.
1803	Jefferson purchases Louisiana Territory.
	Supreme Court hears *Marbury v. Madison*.
1804	Jefferson is reelected.
	Lewis and Clark explore Louisiana Territory.
1807	The Chesapeake Affair incites war fever.
	Congress passes the Embargo Act.
1808	James Madison is elected president of the United States.
1809	Congress repeals the Embargo Act.
	Congress passes the Non-Intercourse Act.
1811	The Battle of Tippecanoe.
1812	United States declares war on Great Britain.
	Madison is reelected.
1814	New Englanders discuss secession at Hartford Convention.
	Treaty of Ghent ends War of 1812.
1816	Congress passes the Tariff of 1816.
	James Monroe is elected president.
1818	General Andrew Jackson invades Florida.
1819	The Panic of 1819 ends the Era of Good Feelings.
	Spain cedes Florida to the United States.
	The House passes the Tallmadge Amendment.
	The *McCulloch v. Maryland* ruling increases the power of federal government.
	Dartmouth College v. Woodward rules that states cannot amend legal contracts.

1820	The Missouri Compromise is proposed by Henry Clay.
	Monroe is reelected.
1823	John Quincy Adams devises the Monroe Doctrine.
1824	The *Gibbons v. Ogden* ruling gives Congress authority to regulate interstate commerce.

Major Figures

John Adams A prominent Bostonian lawyer, Adams first became famous for defending the British soldiers accused of murdering five civilians in the Boston Massacre. He was a delegate from Massachusetts in the Continental Congresses where he rejected proposals for home rule. He served as vice president to George Washington and was president of the United States from 1797–1801.

John C. Calhoun Even though Calhoun served as vice president to both John Quincy Adams and Andrew Jackson, he also led the movement to nullify the 1828 Tariff of Abominations in South Carolina. Shortly after Congress passed the tariff, he wrote *The South Carolina Exposition* that urged South Carolina legislators to declare the tax null and void in the state. The Exposition and Nullification Crisis was the greatest challenge the nation had yet faced and illustrated the emerging sectional differences. Calhoun is also regarded as one of America's finest political theorists.

Henry Clay Also known as the Great Pacificator, this Kentuckian served as speaker of the House of Representatives, secretary of state to John Quincy Adams, and later as a U.S. senator. He was the father of the American System to promote higher tariffs and internal improvements at government expense. He earned his nickname for devising both the Missouri Compromise of 1820 and the compromise Tariff of 1833 to end the nullification crisis. In 1834, Clay allied himself with Daniel Webster of New England to form the Whigs, a progressive new political party for internal improvements, limited westward expansion, and reform. Even though he never served as president (he ran and lost three times), historians regard him as one of America's greatest statesmen.

William Henry Harrison A former governor of Indiana Territory and an army general, Harrison rose to national stardom when he defeated the Northwest Confederacy at the Battle of Tippecanoe in 1811. He became the first Whig president when he defeated incumbent Martin Van Buren in the election of 1840. Harrison's election marked the beginning of the Second Party System in American politics (Whigs vs. Democrats), but he died after less than a month in office. He was also the grandfather of Gilded Age president Benjamin Harrison.

Andrew Jackson Hero of the Battle of New Orleans and of the Creek War, Jackson entered the national political arena when he challenged John Quincy Adams for the presidency in 1824. After a controversial loss, he ran again in 1828 and won. His presidency was plagued by one crisis after another, from the Bank War to the Nullification Crisis, to the forced removal of thousands of Native Americans from their homes. Jackson's presidency has become associated with a surge in democracy, westward expansion, and a strengthened federal government.

John Jay Coauthor of *The Federalist Papers*, Jay worked tirelessly to convince Anti-Federalist New Yorkers to ratify the Constitution. He served as the first Chief Justice of the Supreme Court and became one of the most hated men in American after he negotiated Jay's Treaty in 1794 with Great Britain.

Thomas Jefferson A Virginia planter and lawyer, Jefferson proved himself to be invaluable to the revolutionary cause when he drafted the Declaration of Independence in 1776, which justified American independence from Great Britain. He later served as the first secretary of state under President George Washington and as vice president to John Adams. He was elected president in 1800 and 1804.

James Madison Originally a Federalist, Madison supported the ratification of the Constitution to replace the Articles of Confederation, and wrote some of the best essays on American government and republicanism as coauthor of *The Federalist Papers*. He also personally drafted the Bill of Rights, afraid that the Constitution might be amended if handed to a committee. After ratification, he began supporting southern and western agrarian interests as a Democratic-Republican. He coauthored the Virginia and Kentucky Resolutions with Thomas Jefferson in 1798 while in retirement in Virginia. He later reentered politics and was eventually elected president in 1808 and again in 1812. As the fourth president, Madison promoted the development of southern and western agriculture as his predecessor and friend Thomas Jefferson had. He repealed the Embargo Act, but supported the Non-Intercourse Act and Macon's Bill No. 2. He led the United States in the War of 1812.

James Monroe Without any serious Federalist competition, the Democratic-Republican Monroe was elected president in 1816 and ushered in the Era of Good Feelings. An excellent administrator, Monroe bolstered the federal government and supported internal improvements. His first term went so well that he ran virtually uncontested in the election of 1820. The good times ended, however, during the Missouri Crisis of 1819 and 1820, which split the United States into North and South. He is most famous for his 1823 Monroe Doctrine, warning European Powers to stay out of the affairs of Latin America.

John Marshall Chief justice of the Supreme Court, Marshall was instrumental in establishing judicial review, in which the Supreme Court rules whether laws passed by Congress are constitutional. Marshall also served as a captain in the Continental Army under George Washington and spent the winter in Valley Forge in 1777.

Tecumseh A member of the Shawnee tribe, Tecumseh and his brother, the Prophet, organized many of the tribes in the Mississippi Valley into the Northwest Confederacy to defend their lands from white American settlers. Even though the tribes had legal rights to their lands according to the Indian Intercourse Act of 1790, the Democratic-Republican War Hawks in Congress ordered General William Henry Harrison to wipe out the Confederacy. Tecumseh and his brother were defeated at the Battle of Tippecanoe in 1811.

Suggested Reading

• Bernstein, R.B. *Thomas Jefferson*. New York: Oxford University Press, 2003.

Bernstein's biography provides a fair and unbiased account of a man full of contradictions.

• Newmyer, R. Kent. *John Marshall and the Heroic Age of the Supreme Court*. Baton Rouge: Louisiana State University Press, 2002

This scholarly account details the life of John Marshall and his actions while serving on the Supreme Court.

• Simon, James F. *What Kind of Nation: Thomas Jefferson, John Marshall, and the Epic Struggle to Create a United States*. New York: Simon & Schuster, 2003.

Simon writes about the struggle between Jefferson and Marshall to define the judicial and executive branches of the government.

CHAPTER 5
1800-1824

Jacksonian Democracy: 1824–1848

- The Election of 1824
- The Rise of Mass Democracy
- The Nullification Crisis
- Jackson's Bank War
- Indian Removal
- Van Buren, Harrison, and Tyler
- Manifest Destiny and Polk
- The Mexican-American War

6

National pride surged after the War of 1812 with Great Britain, and Americans began defining their purpose and position in the world more ambitiously than before. Fueled by zeal and optimism, the United States expanded politically, geographically, and culturally. Believing that God had given America a Manifest Destiny to expand from the Atlantic to the Pacific coast, Americans crossed the Appalachians, forded the Mississippi River, and walked or rode in covered wagons westward all the way to California and Oregon by mid-century.

The geographic expansion of the American population coincided with an increase in social and political equality among America's citizens. Americans believed they could change their station in life and that hard work and determination could take them anywhere. This social and political equality, however, did not extend to all Americans, and the escalating issues of sectionalism and slavery would grow increasingly more divisive as mid-century approached. Finally, 1848 saw the rise to prominence of a Whig congressman from Illinois named Abraham Lincoln, whose influence on the country over the next fifteen years was impossible to foresee at the time.

The Election of 1824

Four major candidates contended for the presidency in the election of 1824:

- **John Quincy Adams**, the son of former president John Adams, represented New England.

- **Andrew Jackson**, the champion of the common man, drew widespread support from the West and South.

- William Crawford, a southern planter, advocated states' rights.

- **Henry Clay,** who championed the American System, appealed to wealthier Americans.

The fact that four candidates had decided to run for the presidency was proof that the Missouri Compromise of 1820, which allowed slavery in the South and prohibited it north of the 36° 30' parallel, had replaced the Era of Good Feelings with sectionalism and divisiveness. Americans held many differing views regarding the direction in which the country should move.

THE AMERICAN SYSTEM

Henry Clay ran on the **"American System"** platform, which sought to improve the fledgling United States by:

- Promoting internal improvements such as building canals and national roads

- Raising **protective tariffs** on foreign goods to help domestic manufacturers

- Establishing a **Bank of the United States** to stabilize the economy

The American System dominated the election of 1824. Candidates Clay and Adams both endorsed the system, but Jackson opposed it.

ADAMS'S CORRUPT BARGAIN

After a vicious campaign, Jackson emerged as the most popular candidate, garnering 99 electoral votes to Adams's 84, Crawford's 41, and Clay's 37. But since no single candidate received the necessary clear majority in the Electoral College, it fell to the House of Representatives to decide which of the top three candidates would become the next president. As speaker of the House, Clay threw his support to Adams in exchange for becoming the next secretary of state. Clay's support brought Adams to the presidency, but many Americans joined Jackson in denouncing Clay and Adams's **"corrupt bargain**."His reputation ruined, Adams had very little influence during his four years as president.

The Rise of Mass Democracy

By the 1830s, most states had eliminated voting qualifications such as literacy tests and property ownership, so that all white males could vote. As a result of this trend toward **universal manhood suffrage,** the number of voters increased dramatically, from 350,000 in 1824 to more than 2.5 million by 1840.

THE ELECTION OF 1828

By 1828, political leaders such as Adams and Clay, who promoted policies focused on internal improvements to the country, had split from Jackson's Democratic-Republicans (eventually to become known simply as Democrats) and formed their own National Republican Party. Adams and Jackson faced off once again in the presidential election of 1828. Not surprisingly, the tainted Adams lost, winning only New England.

POLITICS OF PERSONALITY

Jackson believed that his landslide victory in 1828 had given him a mandate from the people to do whatever he deemed right. As a result, he greatly expanded the powers of the presidency. For example, Jackson vetoed bills he personally disliked, unlike previous presidents who had only vetoed bills they thought unconstitutional. Jackson also strengthened the federal government at the expense of individual state governments.

THE SPOILS SYSTEM

Jackson believed that political power should rest with the people in a democracy. He used this belief as a justification for replacing many career civil servants in the capital with his own political allies. This action marked the rise of the Spoils System in nineteenth-century American politics, a system in which presidents award the best appointments in government to their friends and supporters. While previous presidents had practiced this system to a lesser degree, Jackson was the first to publicly attempt to justify and defend it.

> Unlike his predecessors, Jackson relied less on his cabinet secretaries than he did on a set of close friends and allies that critics dubbed his "Kitchen Cabinet." Jackson rarely sought advice outside of this inner circle. In fact, midway through his first administration, Jackson completely reorganized his cabinet and removed most of the secretaries he had originally appointed.

The Nullification Crisis

The tariff issue once again shot to the political foreground in 1828, when Congress unexpectedly passed the Tariff of 1828, setting duties on imported goods at nearly 50 percent, a great increase from the current duties. Jackson actually disliked the tariff and knew it would be unpopular but had pushed for its passage before his election to the presidency to further discredit Adams. As soon as he entered the White House, however, the so-called **Tariff of Abominations** (the Tariff of 1828) became his problem.

A tariff is a duty or tax on goods imported from abroad. Northerners generally wanted tariffs in order to protect their manufactured goods from imports. Southerners did not want high tariffs because they relied heavily on trade with Britain. As a result, tariffs became one of the major sectional issues in the years before the Civil War.

CALHOUN'S SOUTH CAROLINA EXPOSITION

As a westerner, Jackson had no love for the new tariff, which hurt the agricultural South and West, but he didn't seek its repeal either. Jackson's vice president, **John C. Calhoun**, hated the Tariff of Abominations so much that he anonymously encouraged his home state to nullify the law in a pamphlet published in 1828 called *The South Carolina Exposition and Protest*. Calhoun argued that states could nullify any act of Congress they deemed unconstitutional because the states had created the central government and therefore had greater power. Calhoun believed the South Carolina legislature should nullify the new tariff because the tariff protected textile manufacturers in northern states and hurt southern cotton-producing states when the price of cotton abroad rose.

Calhoun expanded upon Thomas Jefferson and James Madison's 1798 **Virginia and Kentucky Resolutions** when writing The South Carolina Exposition. Like his democratic predecessors, Calhoun also drew on the Compact Theory of Government, which states that there must be agreement between those who govern and those who are governed, to defend the supremacy of states' rights over the power of the federal government. Southerners would use this same argument to justify secession in 1860 and 1861.

CHAPTER 6
1824–1848

THE TARIFF OF 1832

Though the southern states protested vehemently against the Tariff of 1828, the tariff generated large revenues that helped the government pay many of its debts. With federal finances in better shape, Jackson signed the lower **Tariff of 1832**. Calhoun and South Carolinians, however, continued to protest. Although they despised the tax itself, they resented federal supremacy over the states even more. Consequently, legislators in South Carolina declared the new tariff null and void in the state and even threatened to secede if Jackson tried to enforce tax collection.

The Nullification Proclamation

Jackson was outraged at South Carolina's challenge to the authority of the federal government, and he issued his own **Nullification Proclamation** denying any state's right to nullify federal laws. Moreover, he declared nullification treasonous and threatened to hang the nullifiers himself. He organized a corps of army troops loyal to the Union and then railroaded the **Force Bill** through Congress in 1833, justifying the use of military force to collect tariff duties in South Carolina.

The Compromise Tariff of 1833

Just as violence seemed imminent, the "Great Compromiser," **Henry Clay**, proposed and passed the **Compromise Tariff of 1833**, which reduced tariff rates over the next ten years. Since no other state supported South Carolina, state legislators reluctantly decided to accept the new tariff. They did, however, nullify the Force Bill out of spite.

Jackson's Bank War

By 1832, the **Second Bank of the United States** had become the most important financial institution in the nation. Many Americans, however, hated the bank, especially farmers and land speculators who could not repay their loans after the agricultural market crashed during the Panic of 1819. Jackson himself had lost most of his money in 1819 and blamed the country's financial problems on the bank.

Henry Clay, afraid that Jackson and the Democrats might not renew the bank's charter in 1836, when it would otherwise expire, attempted to renew the charter several years early, in 1832. Clay also hoped to make the bank a key issue in the presidential election later that year. Congress passed a bill renewing the bank's charter, but Jackson vetoed it. Jackson believed that the strong national bank:

- Unfairly stifled competition from smaller state banks and private banks

- Violated the Constitution, which states that only the federal government could regulate currency

- Encouraged speculation that eventually caused panics and depressions

- Oppressed the poor while making rich financiers even wealthier

THE ELECTION OF 1832

Clay succeeded in making the bank one of the most important issues in the election of 1832. Three candidates contended for the presidency that year:

- Andrew Jackson ran on the Democratic ticket against the bank and lower tariffs.

- Henry Clay, representing the National Republicans, pressed for the bank, higher tariffs, and internal improvements.

- William Wirt, running for the **Anti-Masonic Party**, opposed the Order of the Masons.

Clay's plan to win the presidency by supporting the bank back-fired. Jackson won the election easily with the votes of millions of recently enfranchised voters in the poorer areas of the West and South who hated the bank.

Although never a major party, the Anti-Masonic Party was the first third party to run a candidate in a presidential election and the first to specify its aims in a detailed party platform. The Anti-Masonic Party's primary objective was to end the Freemasonry movement, a secret society with religious overtones found throughout the United States. The party tried to capitalize on the public's fear of conspiracies and secret societies at the time.

Jackson Kills the Bank

Jackson interpreted his sweeping victory as a mandate from the people to destroy the Bank of the United States, and he did so by withdrawing all federal money and depositing it into smaller state banks instead. Afraid that the bank's death would encourage investors to over-speculate in western lands, valuing them more than they were worth, Jackson also issued a **Specie Circular** in 1836 that required all land to be purchased with hard currency.

Indian Removal

Jackson, bowing to pressure from western settlers, convinced Congress to pass the **Indian Removal Act** in 1830, which authorized the forced relocation of tens of thousands of Native Americans to the "Great American Desert" west of the Mississippi, a land so inhospitable that most believed no white settlers would ever want to settle there.

NATIVE AMERICAN RESISTANCE

The Native American tribes affected by the Indian Removal Act did not move quietly. The U.S. army encountered some of the heaviest resistance from the Fox and Sauk in the Old Northwest region near the Great Lakes. Chief Black Hawk and his warriors resisted resettlement for two years until American troops ended the **Black Hawk War** in 1832. The Seminoles in Florida resisted relocation for seven years in the **Seminole War**.

Cherokees Fight the Law

The Cherokee tribe in Georgia also refused to comply with the new law. As one of the so-called Five Civilized Tribes, the Cherokee had actually taken great strides to assimilate into white southern culture. Most worked as farmers and some even owned large slave plantations. Instead of fighting for their homes, however, they challenged the law in court. Chief Justice John Marshall ruled in:

- *Cherokee Nation v. Georgia* in 1831 that the United States could not remove the Cherokee because they legally owned their lands as a separate nation independent from the United States

- *Worcester v. Georgia* in 1832 that Georgia could not force its laws on the independent Cherokee

The Trail of Tears

Jackson blatantly ignored the Court's rulings and forced the Cherokee to cede their lands and relocate to the Arkansas Territory. More than 12,000 Cherokee walked the **"Trail of Tears"** with the Choctaws, Chickasaws, Creeks, and conquered Seminoles. Thousands died from hunger, cold, and disease during this humiliating journey.

Van Buren, Harrison, and Tyler

Jackson, who had become old and weak, declined to run for a third term in 1836. His bold policies against nullification and the central bank had prompted his political opponents to form the new **Whig Party**, led by former National Republican leader Henry Clay. Like the National Republicans, the Whigs supported the American System, promoting internal improvements, creating protective tariffs, and supporting the bank.

ELECTION OF 1836

Four major candidates competed for the White House in 1836:

- **Martin Van Buren**, a Democrat and Jackson's hand-picked successor

- **Daniel Webster**, a prominent statesman from New England and Whig leader

- Hugh Lawson White, a Whig from Tennessee

- **William Henry Harrison**, yet another Whig and a famous war hero

The Whigs ran three candidates against Van Buren in the hopes that one of them could garner enough votes to oust the Jacksonian Democrats from the White House. The three candidates competing against each other, however, merely scattered Whig votes so that none of them had enough to defeat the popular Van Buren. As a result, Van Buren easily defeated his opponents to become the eighth president.

THE PANIC OF 1837

Van Buren's presidency was blighted by the Panic of 1837 and the ensuing depression. Jackson's Specie Circular, issued just before he left office, required the payment of public land to be in gold or silver rather than paper money. This caused a run on banks, especially those in the West, as thousands tried to withdraw their money in gold and silver coins. Commodity prices fell, hundreds

of banks shut down, and millions of Americans found themselves out of work or too poor to farm.

In response, Van Buren forced Congressional Democrats to pass
a **Divorce Bill** to separate federal money from unstable banks
and redeposit it in a new and independent treasury. Van Buren
hoped that such a move would restore Americans' faith in the
economic stability of the government. But the depression only
worsened and contributed to Van Buren's growing unpopularity.

THE HARD CIDER ELECTION OF 1840

The Depression ruined Van Buren's chances of reelection in
1840. Nevertheless, the Democrats nominated him again for
lack of a better candidate. The Whigs, meanwhile, had grown
wiser in the last four years and decided to focus their efforts
on a single candidate instead of three. In the 1840 election,
Democrats nominated Martin Van Buren, and Whigs nominated war hero William Henry Harrison. The Whigs appealed
to common voters in the West and South by touting Harrison as
a log-cabin-born, hard-cider-guzzling frontiersman. This strategy
worked, and Harrison easily defeated Van Buren, much to the
jubilation of Henry Clay and Daniel Webster. Yet, fewer than
thirty days after taking the oath of office, Harrison died.

> It was believed that Harrison died from pneumonia contracted
> while delivering a two-hour speech in the cold on his inauguration
> day. He had refused to wear a jacket to give his speech, despite the
> temperatures, and was the first president to die in office.

JOHN TYLER'S PRESIDENCY

Harrison's relatively unknown running mate, **John Tyler**,
became president and proceeded to pursue his own agenda. Tyler,
a former Democrat who'd only joined the Whig Party to oppose
Jackson, had no love for federally funded internal improvements,
higher protective tariffs, or a national bank. Instead, the new
president tried to reduce tariffs, give more power to the individual states, and even vetoed a Whig bill to revive the Bank of the
United States. Furious at Tyler's betrayal, Whig leaders officially
expelled him from the party in 1842.

Manifest Destiny and Polk

In 1845, a New York newspaper editor wrote, "Our manifest destiny is to overspread the continent allotted by Providence for the free development of our yearly multiplying millions." The American public quickly latched on to **Manifest Destiny** and the belief that Americans had a mandate from God to spread democracy throughout North America. Thousands of settlers poured from the growing urban regions in the East to California, Oregon, and Texas. This belief in Manifest Destiny spread all the way to the highest levels of government, where congressmen and presidents traded, bought, annexed, and even went to war for new lands.

THE WEBSTER-ASHBURTON TREATY

The **Webster-Ashburton Treaty** of 1842 marked the government's first step toward fulfilling America's perceived destiny. The treaty, between the United States and Great Britain, settled the boundary disputes between the United States and Canada over the ore-rich Great Lakes region. It also stipulated that both countries would jointly occupy the Oregon Territory.

TEXAS

Texas declared independence from Mexico in 1836 and immediately requested annexation by the United States. Northern Whigs and others opposed to the expansion of slavery protested the creation of another slave state and blocked the southerners' move to annex Texas. Moreover, Congress had promised noninterference to Mexican officials during the war and thus couldn't legally annex Texas. Mexico, meanwhile, tried several times to retake its rebellious state over the next decade, with no success.

Britain's Plans for Texas

Forced to protect themselves without any assistance from the United States, Texans negotiated trade and security treaties with several European powers. Britain in particular became very interested in Texas because an independent Texas would help them by:

- Halting American expansion

- Weakening the Monroe Doctrine, which might eventually allow Britain to found new colonies in North America

- Providing another source of cotton for British textile manufacturers

ELECTION OF 1844

Texas became the hottest issue in the election of 1844 after American policymakers discovered Britain's plans. The election also focused on Oregon, tariffs, and the increasingly heated slavery issue. The major candidates of the election included:

- Henry Clay, a veteran Whig statesman, who ran on a platform against the annexation of Texas

- **James K. Polk**, a Democratic lawyer and Tennessee planter, who ran on a platform in favor of annexation

- James G. Birney, the new **Liberty Party** candidate, who was an abolitionist and ran on an antislavery platform

Historians often refer to the election of 1844 as the Manifest Destiny Election because candidates focused primarily on westward expansion. The issue of Texas loomed large, and the election also featured the first candidate to run on a platform advocating the abolition of slavery.

Texas Joins the Union

Polk barely won the election, with only 40,000 more popular votes than Clay. Sitting president John Tyler interpreted the victory as a mandate from the people to annex Texas. Before leaving office, Tyler asked Congress in 1845 for a joint resolution to annex Texas. Unlike the usual two-thirds vote of the Senate that was needed to ratify a treaty, the resolution required only a simple majority of each house. The resolution passed, and Texas was added to the Union as a slave state later that year.

Outraged, Mexico immediately withdrew its ambassador to the United States. More trouble arose when the two countries became embroiled in a border dispute. Americans claimed that the Rio Grande River divided Texas from Mexico, whereas Mexicans marked the border at the Nueces River farther north in Texas. Both sent troops to the region, the Americans camping north of the Nueces and the Mexicans to the south of the Rio Grande. War would soon erupt.

THE POLK PRESIDENCY

James K. Polk entered the White House with a three-pronged agenda. He wanted to reduce tariffs, acquire Oregon, and acquire California. Amazingly, he achieved all three goals in only four years' time.

Tariff Reduction. Polk successfully pushed the **Walker Tariff** through Congress in 1846 to reduce general tariff rates from 32 percent to 25 percent.

Oregon. Although the United States had jointly occupied the Oregon Territory with Great Britain for several decades, Polk wanted sole ownership of Oregon for the United States, all the way to the southern border of Alaska at the 54° 40' parallel. Most Americans supported the move for all of Oregon, particularly considering that nearly 5,000 Americans had settled there after crossing the continent on the perilous **Oregon Trail**.

Polk pressured Britain to relinquish Oregon to the point of threatening war, but eventually signed the compromise **Oregon Treaty** in 1846 to split Oregon at the forty-ninth parallel. Britain took all of present-day British Columbia while the United States took all the territory that eventually became Washington State, Oregon, Idaho, and parts of Montana.

California. Polk's greatest ambition of all was to add California to the United States. Polk particularly desired the glittering San Francisco Bay, which could open the United States to lucrative trade deals with Asia. Unfortunately for the president, Mexico had strong territorial claims to California. Polk's designs on California, as well as the U.S. troops stationed in Texas, led to conflict with Mexico once again.

The Mexican-American War

President Polk sent envoy John Slidell to Mexico in 1845, hoping to smooth relations with Mexico, resolve the Texas issue, and buy California. The president authorized Slidell to purchase California and New Mexico for a total of $25 million. Mexico, of course, refused the low offer and sent Slidell back to Washington. Undoubtedly knowing full well that Mexico would refuse the offer, Polk had simultaneously sent adventurer **John C. Frémont** to California, ostensibly on a scientific survey mission. At the same time, Polk sent several U.S. Navy ships to the California coast. General **Zachary Taylor** and 2,000 troops moved from their position north of the Nueces River and encamped along the northern shores of the Rio Grande River in disputed territory.

POLK ASKS FOR WAR

In April of 1846, Mexican troops crossed the Rio Grande and attacked Taylor's men camped in disputed territory. Immediately after receiving news of the Mexican attack, Polk "reluctantly" requested that Congress declare war. After much debate, Congress eventually acquiesced. As soon as Congress formally declared war the following month, U.S. forces defeated the Mexicans quickly and easily. In a little over a year and a half:

- Frémont and the navy seized California.

- American troops seized most of present day New Mexico and Arizona.

- Taylor seized all of northern Mexico after defeating an overwhelming Mexican force at the Battle of Buena Vista.

- General Winfield Scott seized Mexico City in September 1847 to end the war.

THE TREATY OF GUADALUPE-HIDALGO

American and Mexican diplomats signed the **Treaty of Guadalupe-Hidalgo** in 1848 to end the war. In the treaty:

- Mexico ceded California and most of present-day New Mexico, Arizona, Nevada, Colorado, and Wyoming to the United States.

- Mexico abandoned its claims to Texas.

- The Rio Grande River was established as the border between Texas and Mexico.

- The United States generously agreed to pay Mexico 15 million dollars for all lands acquired.

LINCOLN'S "SPOT RESOLUTIONS"

Despite the American victory and the enormous territorial gains that came with it, Polk faced severe criticism for the war in Washington. Whig congressman **Abraham Lincoln** continually badgered Polk about the exact spot where the Mexicans had engaged Taylor. These **"spot" resolutions** damaged Polk's reputation and led many to believe that the president had intentionally provoked the Mexicans in order to seize California.

> *The Mexican War gave future Civil War commanders such as Robert E. Lee, Ulysses S. Grant, Stonewall Jackson, and William Tecumseh Sherman valuable experience on the battlefield. In fact, many of them served side by side in campaigns in Mexico and the West.*

THE LEGACY OF THE MEXICAN-AMERICAN WAR

The vast majority of Americans had supported the war despite the $98 million price tag and the loss of approximately 12,000 men. However, the war was never perceived as a moral crusade based on the defense of democratic principles, because the United States hadn't fought for independence, freedom for oppressed peoples, or to save democracy. Rather, Americans had gone to war primarily in the name of Manifest Destiny, to expand and acquire more land. At war's end, most Americans felt jubilant that the United States finally spread from coast to coast. The ever-present issue of the expansion of slavery into the new territories, however, would quickly sour the spoils of victory.

Was Polk justified in asking Congress to declare war on Mexico, or was his request merely a thinly veiled attempt to seize more western territory?

President James K. Polk engineered the Mexican–American War of 1846–1848 in order to seize more western territory for the United States. While no one disputes that Mexico and the United States were on a collision course over which country would have control of the Texas territory, Polk deliberately inflamed the situation to justify military action and to seize land in present-day California and New Mexico. Polk's motives are clearly demonstrated by his expansion of the scope of the war into lands well outside the borders of Texas, and in his presidential-campaign promises. Even members of Congress seriously questioned Polk's motivations, and when a young congressman named Abraham Lincoln grilled him over the incident, it ended any chance Polk had for reelection to a second term. All of these issues place the legitimacy of the Mexican–American War in serious doubt.

The future of the Texas territory was the central issue of the election of 1844. Texans had won their independence from Mexico in 1836 and had petitioned for admittance to the United States, but annexation had not been approved. Ex-president Martin Van Buren was expected to win the Democratic Party's nomination for president. Van Buren opposed the annexation of Texas, fearing it would divide the party and invite war with Mexico. When these views became clear at the Democratic convention, many southern delegates, who desperately wanted a new southern proslavery state added to the Union, were furious and threw their support to James Polk, an outspoken expansionist. Polk ran a campaign that highlighted his determination to expand the United States from the Atlantic to the Pacific, and his message won him the election. Congress correctly perceived public opinion and approved the annexation of Texas in the days before Polk officially took office. However, annexation by the United States did not put an end to the issue of Texas.

Mexico and the United States had long been in dispute over the territory of Texas. White Texans had petitioned the U.S. Congress for annexation as early as 1836. Mexico, however, still considered

Student Essay

the Lone Star Republic to be a territory in revolt. By the time the United States annexed Texas in 1845, Mexico's claims, at least in the eyes of Americans, had long since expired. Therefore, the United States proceeded to seize all of Texas down to the Rio Grande River. This sparked a new conflict, since Mexico claimed the southern border of Texas was located farther north, at the Nueces River. In response, Polk ordered a small American military force to advance south and take up station along the north bank of the Rio Grande. This action provoked Mexican forces, which crossed the Rio Grande on April 24, 1846, and attacked a small American force, killing eleven. When news arrived in Washington, D.C., that Taylor's troops were under attack, Polk asked Congress to declare full-scale war upon Mexico. The incident suggests that Polk wanted the war to happen, as a declaration of war was not really required to settle a single small battle.

Polk's true intentions quickly became clear. Just days after war was declared, the U.S. military seized the San Francisco Bay area along with other territories in California. Later, the Treaty of Guadalupe–Hidalgo, which ended the war in 1848, forced Mexico to give up all of California as well as most of present-day New Mexico, Arizona, Nevada, Colorado, and Wyoming. Though a huge territorial gain for the United States and a popular victory for Polk, it had little to do with the small skirmish along the Rio Grande that started the war. This demonstrates the breadth of Polk's expansionist agenda, which was completely in line with the Manifest Destiny platform upon which he was elected. Obviously, Polk's goals included far more than just Texas, and the war with Mexico was a convenient way of achieving them.

The entire affair was heavily questioned in Washington. In particular, Congressman Abraham Lincoln expressed doubt about Polk's motives in his so-called "Spot Resolutions." In these resolutions, Lincoln badgered the Polk administration over exactly where Taylor's troops had been "attacked." This severely hurt Polk politically and sparked additional debates about whether the war had been justified. Expansionism had not factored into Polk's public justification of the war, which made his actions appear misleading. Polk became symbolic of America's unquenchable thirst for land and convinced some that the nation was prepared to stoop to any low to expand its territory.

It is highly doubtful that the chain of events surrounding the Mexican–American War was a coincidence. The speed with which Polk pursued territories outside of Texas once the war was underway supports this conclusion, as does the Manifest Destiny platform on which he was elected. Congressional concerns over the war's justification confirm the suspicious nature of Polk's actions. The new western territories acquired under the Polk administration as a result of the Mexican–American War substantially expanded the nation. However, Polk's public justification of the war was essentially deceptive. As a result, Polk's political career was over, and nations around the world began to see the United States in a much different, and very negative, light.

Test Questions and Answers

1. How did democracy expand in the 1820s?

- Most of the property-based voting qualifications were abolished between 1800 and 1820, giving all white males the right to vote.
- Presidential candidates were nominated and no longer appointed.

2. What deeper sectional issues lay at the heart of South Carolina's Nullification Crisis? What did the crisis mean for the future?

- South Carolinians and most southerners feared northerners wanted to abolish slavery.
- The crisis foreshadowed the Civil War.

3. What principles did the various parties represent? What did it mean politically that third parties began contending in presidential elections?

- The Democrats represented the common man's needs and reflected the broadening of democracy.
- The National Republicans emphasized internal improvements, higher tariffs, and industrialization to strengthen the economy.
- The emergence of third parties signified the growing power of special interests groups ranging from the Whigs who opposed Jackson to the Liberty Party that represented Abolitionists.

4. Americans have had a sense of destiny in their nation building from the beginning. How did this sense of mission relate to the concept of Manifest Destiny?

- Manifest Destiny was the belief that Americans were divinely ordained to spread from the Atlantic to the Pacific Coast.

- Americans believed that it was their right to conquer the continent, and their victories over the British, Spanish, natives, and Mexicans reinforced their views that God had chosen them to rule and control the land.

- Since John Winthrop had delivered his "City upon a Hill" sermon to the Puritans, Americans had embraced a mission to first create a Zion of religious perfectionism and then to build a temple to Democratic absolutism.

5. Did most Americans support the Mexican War in 1846?

- Most Americans believed that the United States was justified in going to war with Mexico.

- Because of the principles of Manifest Destiny, Americans believed that God had ordained them to control the territory and bring a democratic government to the area.

Timeline

1824	The disputed presidential election of 1824 is dominated by the American System.
1825	House of Representatives chooses Adams for the presidency.
1828	Congress passes the "Tariff of Abominations."
	Andrew Jackson is elected president.
	John C. Calhoun publishes *The South Carolina Exposition*.
1830	Congress passes the Indian Removal Act.
1832	Jackson thwarts attempts to recharter the Bank of the United States.
	Congress passes the Tariff of 1832.
	Jackson is reelected.
	Jackson issues the Nullification Proclamation.
	The Black Hawk War ends one of the most destructive conflicts between pioneers and Native Americans.
1833	Congress passes Tariff of 1833.
	Jackson withdraws federal money from the Bank of the United States.
	Congress passes the Force Bill.
1834	The Whig Party forms.
1836	The Bank of the United States' charter expires.
	Texas declares independence from Mexico.
	185 Texans fight a 4,000-man Mexican army in the Battle of the Alamo.
	Jackson issues Specie Circular.
	Martin Van Buren is elected president.
1837	Thousands withdraw money from banks in the Panic of 1837.
	Congress refuses to annex Texas.
1838	The army forcibly removes the Cherokee on the "Trail of Tears."
1840	William Henry Harrison is elected president.
	The Liberty Party forms.

CHAPTER 6
1824–1848

1841	William Henry Harrison dies a month after becoming president.
	Vice President John Tyler becomes president.
1842	The United States and Britain sign the Webster–Ashburton Treaty.
1844	James K. Polk is elected president.
1845	The United States annexes Texas.
1846	Congress passes the Walker Tariff.
	The United States resolves the dispute over Oregon with Great Britain.
	The Mexican War erupts.
	John Frémont seizes California.
1847	Gen. Winfield Scott captures Mexico City.
1848	The United States and Mexico sign the Treaty of Guadalupe–Hidalgo.

Major Figures

John Quincy Adams Son of President John Adams, Adams served as James Monroe's secretary of state, and later ran against Andrew Jackson for the presidency in 1824. Because neither he nor Jackson received enough electoral votes to become president, the election was thrown to the House of Representatives. Speaker of the House Henry Clay supported Adams, possibly in exchange for the position of secretary of state. This "corrupt bargain" tainted Adams's presidency and rendered him politically impotent during his four years in office.

John C. Calhoun Even though Calhoun served as vice president to both John Quincy Adams and Andrew Jackson, he also led the movement to nullify the 1828 Tariff of Abominations in South Carolina. Shortly after Congress passed the tariff, he wrote *The South Carolina Exposition* that urged South Carolina legislators to declare the tax null and void in the state. The Exposition and Nullification Crisis was the greatest challenge the nation had yet faced and illustrated the emerging sectional differences. Calhoun is also regarded as one of America's finest political theorists.

Henry Clay Also known as the Great Pacificator, this Kentuckian served as speaker of the House of Representatives, secretary of state to John Quincy Adams, and later as a U.S. senator. Clay was the father of the American System, which promoted higher tariffs and internal improvements at government expense. He earned his nickname for devising both the Missouri Compromise of 1820 and the Compromise Tariff of 1833 to end the nullification crisis. In 1834 he allied himself with Daniel Webster of New England to form the Whigs, a progressive new political party that stood for internal improvements, limited westward expansion, and reform. Even though he never served as president (he ran and lost four times), historians regard him as one of America's greatest statesmen.

John Frémont Within days of Congress declaring war on Mexico in 1846, Frémont seized control of the government of California and declared it an independent country. He then immediately petitioned Congress to annex California. Many accused him of being an agent of James K. Polk and believed his presence in California to have been more than a coincidence. He later ran for president against James Buchanan and Millard Fillmore in 1856: the first presidential candidate for the fledgling Republican party.

William Henry Harrison A former governor of Indiana Territory and army general, Harrison defeated incumbent Martin Van Buren in the election of

1840. His election marked the beginning of the Second Party System in American politics (Whigs vs. Democrats). Sadly, he died after less than a month in office. He was also the grandfather of Gilded Age president Benjamin Harrison.

Andrew Jackson Hero of the Battle of New Orleans and of the Creek War, General Jackson entered the national political arena when he challenged John Quincy Adams for the presidency in 1824. After a controversial loss, he ran again in 1828 and won. His presidency was plagued by one crisis after another, from the Bank War to the Nullification Crisis, to the forced removal of thousands of Native Americans from their homes. Jackson's presidency is associated with a surge in democracy, westward expansion, and a strengthened federal government.

Abraham Lincoln A former lawyer from Illinois, Lincoln became the sixteenth president of the United States in the election of 1860. Because he was a Republican and associated with the abolitionist cause, his election prompted South Carolina to become the first state to secede from the Union. Lincoln believed that the states had legally never truly left the Union, but fought the war until the South surrendered unconditionally. He proposed the Ten-Percent Plan for Reconstruction in 1863, but was assassinated by John Wilkes Booth before he could carry out his plans.

James K. Polk An expansionist Democrat from Kentucky, Polk was elected president on a Manifest Destiny platform in 1844. During his four years in office, he lowered the protective tariff, revived the independent treasury, acquired Oregon, and seized California in the Mexican War. Many critics past and present have accused him of purposefully provoking war with Mexico as an excuse to annex everything between California and Texas.

Zachary Taylor A hero of the Mexican War, Taylor became the second and last Whig president in 1848. He campaigned without a solid platform to avoid controversy over the westward expansion of slavery in the Mexican cession. He died after only two years in office and was replaced by Millard Fillmore.

John Tyler The first president who was not elected, Tyler entered the White House after the death of William Henry Harrison. He had originally been a Democrat, but joined the Whigs in the 1830s because he couldn't stand President Andrew Jackson's autocratic leadership style. His political ideologies never really changed, however, and he consistently shot down most Whig legislation during his four years in office. To Henry Clay's and

Daniel Webster's consternation, he refused to revive the Bank of the United States, and disapproved of funding internal improvements with federal money, though he did pass the protective Tariff of 1842. Outraged, the Whigs kicked him out of the party before the presidential election of 1844. In his final days as president, Tyler succeeded in annexing Texas.

Martin Van Buren   Former secretary of state to Andrew Jackson, Van Buren was elected president on the Democratic ticket in 1836. Unfortunately for him, his years in office were plagued by a depression after the financial Panic of 1837. Believing that federal funds in smaller banks had made the economy worse, Van Buren pushed the Divorce Bill through Congress to create an independent treasury. William Henry Harrison soundly defeated him in the election of 1840. He also ran as the Free-Soil Party candidate in the election of 1848.

Daniel Webster   A senator from New England, Webster was an ardent proponent of the American System. He was a leading statesman in his day, and eventually teamed up with Henry Clay in 1834 to form the new Whig Party. As Whigs, he and Clay campaigned for progressive new reforms and limited westward expansion.

CHAPTER 6
1824–1848

Suggested Reading

• Ehle, John. *Trail of Tears: The Rise and Fall of the Cherokee Nation.* New York: Anchor Books, 1989.

This work depicts the Cherokee Nation, mainly under Jackson's administration, and its forced march from Georgia to Arkansas. Ehle lays bare the brutality of southern white Americans in their desire to remove the Cherokee, despite the tribe's adaptation to the white southern way of life.

• Johanssen, Robert W. *To the Halls of the Montezumas: The Mexican War in the American Imagination.* New York: Oxford University Press, 1988.

The Mexican War was the first war to be fully covered by American newspapers. Johanssen relies on these newspaper accounts, as well as military and travel journals, to show a country fascinated with its own identity and the possibilities presented in the West.

• Remini, Robert. *The Life of Andrew Jackson.* New York: HarperCollins, 1988.

An abridgement to Remini's exhaustive three-volume biography of Jackson, this title effectively portrays the seventh president of the United States from early war years through his presidency.

• Watson, Harry L. *Liberty and Power: The Politics of Jacksonian America.* New York: Hill and Wang, 1990.

More than just an examination of the politics of the Jacksonian era, Watson effectively collects the social, cultural, and economic factors that were present during the time to produce a complete portrayal of the time period.

A Growing Nation: 1820–1860

- The Market Revolution
- Northern Society
- Southern Society
- Revivalism and Utopianism
- The Reform Movement
- The American Renaissance

7

Between 1820 and 1860, the United States developed at a staggering pace, transforming from an underdeveloped nation of mostly backwoods farmers and frontiersmen into an urbanized economic powerhouse. Americans were spreading west during this time, especially to California through the Oregon Trail, and south into Texas. The period was marked by a cultural renaissance, and new American artists and writers were creating major Romantic and Transcendental works. Americans voted in greater numbers than ever before and took an intense interest in national politics, especially in regard to Manifest Destiny and the issue of slavery.

These transformations, rather than foster national unity, helped drive the North and South further and further apart. The market revolution, wage labor, improved transportation, social reforms, and a growing middle class in the North contrasted sharply with the unchanging semifeudalistic social hierarchy in the South. In addition, each of the major debates on slavery and westward expansion shed greater light on the differences between the two parts of the country. As time passed, Americans in the North and South ultimately began viewing themselves as two very different peoples.

The Market Revolution

Between the 1820s and 1860, the **Industrial Revolution** transformed the national economy into a **market-based economy** that was heavily reliant on exportation of goods, especially cotton in the South, and the manufacturing of goods in the North. Internal improvements in transportation as well as new inventions spurred industrial and agricultural production and made transporting goods from one part of the country to another much easier.

THE SOUTHERN AGRICULTURAL REVOLUTION

Although textile manufacturing flourished in Great Britain, it lagged far behind in the United States, primarily because Americans lacked a source of cheap cotton. Southern planters had attempted to grow cotton in the eighteenth century but had almost completely switched to rice and tobacco by the dawn of the nineteenth century-because growing cotton required too much labor.

The Cotton Gin

Inventor **Eli Whitney** made growing cotton more profitable with the automatic **cotton gin**, which he invented in 1793. Whitney's cotton gin vastly reduced the amount of labor required to harvest cotton and transformed the southern economy virtually overnight. Planters quickly abandoned tobacco and rice for the suddenly profitable cotton. Cotton production in turn spurred the construction of textile factories in the North.

> Before Whitney invented the cotton gin, it took one slave an entire day to separate a pound of cotton fibers from the seed. The gin, however, allowed one slave to produce as much as fifty pounds of cotton in a single day. This increase transformed the economic possibilities of the North and the South.

Interchangeable Parts

Several years after inventing the cotton gin, Whitney perfected a system to produce a musket with **interchangeable parts.** Before Whitney, craftsmen had made each individual musket by hand,

and the parts from one musket would not necessarily work in another musket. With interchangeable parts, however, all triggers fit the same model musket, as did all ramrods, all flash pans, all hammers, and all bullets. Manufacturers swiftly applied the concept of interchangeable parts to mass-produce other identical goods.

THE WESTERN AGRICULTURAL REVOLUTION

Many of those new products in turn revolutionized agriculture in the West. John Deere, for example, invented a horse-pulled **steel plow** to replace the difficult oxen-driven wooden plows farmers had used for centuries. The steel plow allowed farmers to till more soil, in less time, for less money, without having to make repairs as often.

McCormick's Mechanical Mower-Reaper

In the 1830s, another inventor, Cyrus McCormick, invented a **mechanical mower-reaper** that quintupled the efficiency of wheat farmers. Often credited as the cotton gin of the West, the mower-reaper allowed farmers to grow large quantities of wheat instead of less profitable corn. As in the South, western farmers raked in huge profits as they acquired more land to plant greater quantities of wheat. More important, farmers for the first time began producing more wheat than the western markets could handle. Rather than letting it go to waste, they sold crop surpluses to the wageworkers in Northeast cities, which in turn helped those cities grow.

> Over time, regional specialization emerged: the West farmed to feed the Northeast, the South grew cotton to ship to the Northeast, and the Northeast produced manufactured goods to sell in the West and South. This specialization would play a very large role in causing the Civil War and determining the victor.

CHAPTER 7
1820–1860

THE TRANSPORTATION REVOLUTION

Western farmers, southern cotton growers, and northern manufacturers all relied on new forms of transportation to move their goods north and south, east and west across the country. Henry Clay's American System inspired state legislatures to construct a number of roads, canals, and other internal improvements to connect the Union.

Roads. Many northern states built turnpikes and toll roads during these years, the most famous being the **Cumberland Road**, or National Road, stretching from Maryland to St. Louis, Missouri, by the time construction finished in 1852. Other well-known roads include the Wilderness Road and the Lancaster Turnpike.

Canals. The **Erie Canal** that spanned the length of New York also helped northerners transport goods from the Great Lakes region to the Hudson River and ultimately the Atlantic. The canal also helped give birth to cities like Chicago, Cleveland, and Detroit, as ships from the Atlantic could now reach far inland. Other northern states built similar canals, usually to link the agricultural West with the industrial East.

Steamboats. The newly invented steamboat permitted fast, two-way traffic on all of these new waterways as well. For the first time in history, mariners didn't have to rely on winds and currents and could travel directly to any port at any time. Within a couple decades of their invention in 1807, steamboats chugged along all the major rivers and canals, and eventually on the high seas.

Railroads. Railroads were another conduit for moving people and goods quickly and cheaply. At first, developers laid tracks primarily along the Eastern seaboard from Virginia to Boston, and in the West from Chicago to Pittsburgh. In the decade prior to the Civil War, however, Americans laid tens of thousands of miles of track, almost all in the North.

In general, only northerners capitalized on the transportation revolution. Although southerners did use steamboats extensively to ship cotton, tobacco, and rice down the Mississippi River, the South boasted very few canals, railroads, or roads. This left the region relatively isolated, a fact of considerable import in the years prior to the Civil War. As a result, although the standard of living improved in all regions during these years, it improved the most in the West and North. Northern manufacturers shipped the bulk of their finished products to the West, while the West grew rich on northern grain purchases.

Northern Society

The market revolution and surge in manufacturing had a tremendous impact on northern society. New York, Boston, Philadelphia, Baltimore, Pittsburgh, and other major cities sometimes tripled or even quadrupled in size between 1820 and 1860 as people left their farms to find work in urban areas. Smaller towns also experienced population growth during these years.

THE WAGE LABOR SYSTEM

As northerners continued building factories, they needed more and more workers to tend the machinery. Rather than learning a trade skill as most workers had in the past, these day laborers worked alongside scores of others, feeding or regulating a machine for hourly pay under harsh conditions. Workers toiled in textile factories for as many as sixteen hours a day, six or seven days a week. Although wealthy business owners loved the cheap labor, wage laborers suffered from poor working conditions.

*Some factories such as the **Lowell Mills** in Massachusetts employed only girls and young women. These factories, which provided room and board, attempted to "moralize" the women with heavy doses of religious preaching and strict discipline. Factory owners tended to employ young children, or "grease monkeys," because the children could easily maneuver through the large machines.*

Strikes and Reforms

Some workers chose to unite and strike in the 1830s and 1840s to protest the inhumane conditions and hours they were forced to work. The strikes caused such a stir in the national press that the government eventually took action. In 1840, for example, President Martin Van Buren established a ten-hour working day for all federal employees. Two years later, the Massachusetts Supreme Court legalized trade unions in the landmark 1842 decision *Commonwealth v. Hunt*. Ultimately, despite the exploitation of early wage laborers, the shift away from craftsmanship toward wage labor helped give rise to a substantial and powerful middle class.

GERMAN AND IRISH IMMIGRATION

Mass immigration from Ireland and Germany was another factor in the urbanization phenomenon. More than 100,000 Irish came to the United States every year in the late 1840s and 1850s to escape the Potato Famine in Ireland, which ultimately killed more than a million people. Most of these immigrants settled in New York, Boston, and later Chicago, but Irish districts emerged in every major northern city. Germans also came en masse to the United States during the same period to escape political persecution in central Europe. These German immigrants generally had more money than the Irish and therefore mostly settled outside the congested cities.

Nativism and the Know-Nothings

A significant number of native-born Americans resented the influx of Germans and Irish. These **"nativists"** considered the Irish and Germans ignorant and inferior human beings, incapable of understanding democracy or assimilating into mainstream American culture. Many Protestants also hated the Germans and the Irish for their Catholic beliefs. The anti-immigration American Party, or **Know-Nothing Party**, was popular among nativists in the 1850s.

> People in the secretive American Party became known as the "Know-Nothings" because they usually claimed not to know anything when questioned about the group. The party grew in the 1840s, reaching its peak in 1855 with forty-three congressional representatives, but soon declined and ceased to be a major political force after 1860.

Southern Society

Although the North and West experienced dramatic social changes, the South for the most part did not. Rather, the southern social fabric remained relatively unchanged between 1820 and 1860 because of the region's reliance on cotton production. Cotton production proved so profitable after the invention of the cotton gin that by 1860, the South produced 75 percent of Britain's cotton supply.

SOUTHERN SOCIAL HIERARCHY

Instead of evolving socially as the North had, the South continued to adhere to an archaic semi-feudalistic social order, which consisted of wealthy planter elites, slave-owning farmers, poor landless whites, and slaves.

Wealthy white plantation owners controlled the southern legislatures, represented the South in Congress, and had some of the largest fortunes in the country. Next came the white landowning subsistence farmers assisted by their one or two family slaves, followed by poor landless whites, who composed the vast majority of the southern population. Black slaves, of course, formed the base of the social hierarchy.

Contrary to popular belief, only one out of every four southern males owned slaves in the 1850s. Moreover, these few slave owners usually owned only one or two slaves. The contemporary conception of large southern plantations with hundreds of slaves was in actuality very rare. However, it was undeniable that the southern economy would collapse without this workforce.

JUSTIFYING SLAVERY

Even though few southerners actually owned slaves, all whites firmly believed in the superiority of their social system. Even the poorest whites supported slavery because they dreamed of becoming wealthy slave owners. Whites justified slavery in many ways. Some championed the "paternal" nature of slavery by arguing that slave owners took care of the inferior race as fathers would small children. Others believed that slavery Christianized blacks and saved them from brutal lives as savages in Africa. All southerners, however, preferred their more "humane" southern slavery to the impersonal "wage slavery" in the North.

CHAPTER 7
1820–1860

Revivalism and Utopianism

A new wave or spiritual revivalism spread across America in the early to mid-nineteenth century. A variety of new denominations and utopian sects emerged during these years, including the Methodists, the Baptists, the Shakers, the Mormons, and Millerites, among others.

THE SECOND GREAT AWAKENING

A newfound sense of spirituality deeply affected Americans in the **antebellum period**. This renewed interest in religion, which began with the **Second Great Awakening** around the turn of the nineteenth century, swept across the country primarily as a reactionary response to the Enlightenment and the so-called "Age of Reason" that had inspired thinkers such as Benjamin Franklin, Thomas Jefferson, and Thomas Paine.

Hundreds of preachers, including **Charles Grandison Finney** and Timothy Dwight, set up revivalist camps in rural areas and attracted thousands of converts throughout the country. The converted often became so frenzied that they would roll, jerk, shake, shout, and even bark in excitement.

> *Revivalism had the greatest impact on women. Shut out from politics and most facets of the new economy, women poured their energy into religion and reform. Many believed they could have a positive impact on society by converting their family, friends, and neighbors.*

The Burned-Over District

Named for its abundance of hellfire-and-damnation preaching, the **Burned-Over District** in western New York produced dozens of new denominations, communal societies, and reform movements. This region was also burned-over (or, perhaps more appropriately, burned-*out*) from the economic changes it had undergone since the completion of the Erie Canal and the rapid development of the new market economy. Influenced by so many new ideas, visionaries, and forces, Americans in the Burned-Over District became some of the nation's greatest reform leaders.

Northern Denominations

Not all of the new Christian denominations were so "spirited." Although hellfire-and-damnation sermons appealed mostly to southerners and westerners, many northern denominations came to be highly regarded for their appeal to reason. Unitarians, Presbyterians, and Episcopalians, for example, attracted a huge following because of their belief in a loving God, free will, and denial of original sin.

UTOPIAN MOVEMENTS

In the spirit of the reform movement, more than 100,000 American men, women, and children between 1820 and 1860 searched for alternative lifestyles. Disenchanted with the world around them, utopian seekers aspired to a perfect society.

Mormons

Another new denomination from the Burned-Over District was the Church of Latter Day Saints, or **Mormon** Church. Founded by Ohioan **Joseph Smith** in 1830, Mormons believed God had entrusted them with a new set of scriptures called the Book of Mormon. Because Smith also advocated polygamy, Mormons faced intense hostility and persecution from Protestants throughout the Midwest.

When an angry Illinois mob murdered Smith in 1844, his disciple Brigham Young took charge of the church and led a mass migration to the desert around the Great Salt Lake (then claimed by Mexico). There the Mormons converted the barren lands into an oasis suitable for growing crops. Utah, the territory settled by the Mormons, eventually became a U.S. territory after the Mexican War, but did not become a state until 1896, when Mormons agreed to abandon the practice of polygamy.

Other Utopian Communities

A variety of other utopian communities appeared and disappeared throughout the mid-nineteenth century. These communities included:

- **New Harmony**, a community of roughly 1,000 Americans in Indiana who believed socialistic communities could end poverty. The community collapsed in just a few short years.

- **Brook Farm**, a community in Massachusetts closely affiliated with the Transcendentalist movement, preached harmony with nature and modest living. This community also collapsed within a few years.

- **Oneida Community**, in upstate New York, practiced free love, birth control, and eugenics.

- **The Millerites**, who eventually disbanded after Jesus failed to appear on October 22, 1843, as promised.

- **The Shaker Movement**, located in several states and boasted more than half a million members at its height, ultimately dissolved because believers were forbidden to marry or have sex.

The Reform Movement

Fueled by the Great Awakening, many progressive northerners, women in particular, strived to improve society. They launched a variety of reform movements against prostitution, the consumption of alcohol, and the mistreatment of prisoners and the insane. Other reformers tried to expand women's rights and improve education. Many of these movements actually succeeded in convincing northern state legislatures to enact new laws. Southern states, however, generally lagged behind, remaining socially conservative.

ABOLITIONISM

The abolitionist movement sought to eradicate slavery and quickly became the most visible reform movement during the antebellum period. Prominent northern abolitionists included Theodore Weld, Sojourner Truth, Frederick Douglass, Elijah P. Lovejoy, and **William Lloyd Garrison**, among many others.

Garrison and The Liberator

Garrison attained infamy after first publishing his antislavery newspaper *The Liberator* in 1831 and then cofounding the American Anti-Slavery Society two years later. A radical abolitionist who called for immediate emancipation, Garrison criticized the South so severely that many southern state legislatures issued warrants and bounties for his arrest or capture. Southerners feared Garrison because they incorrectly assumed he'd helped the black preacher **Nat Turner** lead a bloody slave uprising in Virginia the same year *The Liberator* debuted.

Anti-Abolitionism in the North

Not all northerners supported the abolition movement. In fact, many people actually felt ambivalent about emancipation or even opposed it outright. The blossoming trade unions and wageworkers, for example, hated abolitionists because they feared competition for jobs from free blacks. Most public figures and politicians, even Abraham Lincoln, shunned abolitionists for their radicalism and unwillingness to compromise. As a result, abolitionists at first had few friends and many enemies.

> The abolitionist movement became so raucous that the House of Representatives actually passed a *"gag resolution"* in 1836 to squelch all further discussion of slavery. It was this mentality and willingness to ignore a pressing issue that moved the nation toward civil war.

CHAPTER 7 1820–1860

THE TEMPERANCE MOVEMENT

The **temperance movement** sought to ban the manufacture, sale, and consumption of alcohol. By the 1830s, Americans had earned a reputation for hard drinking, especially in the West and South, where settlers endured extreme hardship. Factory owners in the cities also lamented that alcoholism reduced worker output and caused too many on-the-job accidents. Women, moreover, charged that drinking ruined family life and only led to spousal and child abuse. As the new sense of morality spread throughout the country, more and more people campaigned against drinking.

Early Prohibition

The first chapter of the **American Temperance Society** formed in 1826 and blossomed into thousands of nationwide chapters within the following ten years. The society distributed fliers, pamphlets, and illustrations and paraded victims of abuse and reformed alcoholics through towns to preach against consumption.

The movement gained even more fame when T. S. Arthur published his novel *Ten Nights in a Barroom and What I Saw There* about the horrible effects of hard liquor on a previously quaint village. Several cities and states passed laws prohibiting the sale and consumption of alcohol, such as the so-called **Maine Law** in the northeastern state. However, no federal law or proclamation would make the sale or consumption of alcohol illegal until the 1920s.

PROHIBITING PROSTITUTION

Antebellum reformers struck out against prostitution in the rapidly growing industrial cities. Spearheaded almost entirely by upper- and middle-class women, antiprostitution societies fought not only to reduce the number of working girls on the streets but also to reform them. New York women founded the Female Moral Reform Society in 1834, which branched off to hundreds of other cities and towns by 1840. These societies also strove to end prostitution by decreasing demand. Many newspapers, for example, published the names of prostitutes' patrons, while many states enacted laws to punish clients as well as the prostitutes themselves. However, the world's oldest profession continued unabated.

PRISON REFORM

Reformers also launched a campaign to improve prisons. Early-to mid-nineteenth-century prisons often resembled medieval dungeons and usually only held Americans who couldn't repay their debts. Over time, reformers managed to change the system. Debtor prisons gradually began to disappear as Americans realized the barbarity of locking people away for bad luck or circumstances beyond their control. More and more states also prohibited the use of cruel and inhumane punishments. Reformers also succeeded in convincing several state legislatures that governments should use prisons to help reform criminals, not just incarcerate them.

REFORM FOR THE MENTALLY ILL

Insane-asylum reform went hand in hand with prison reform, as most Americans at the time believed that the mentally ill were no better than animals. As a result, prisons contained thousands of mentally ill prisoners. Prison reformer **Dorothea Dix** spearheaded asylum reform by compiling a comprehensive report on the state of the mentally ill in Massachusetts. The report claimed that jailers had chained hundreds of insane women in stalls and cages. Her findings convinced state legislators to establish one of the first asylums devoted entirely to caring for the mentally ill. By the outbreak of the Civil War, nearly thirty states had built similar institutions.

EDUCATION REFORM

Reformers sought to expand public education too. Most nineteenth-century Americans considered public education only fit for the poor. Wealthier Americans could, of course, pay for their children to attend private primary schools and secondary academies, but they loathed the idea of paying higher taxes to educate the poor.

Over the course of the antebellum period, more and more cities and states acknowledged that public education would expand democracy, improve productivity, and make better citizens. For example, **Horace Mann**, the secretary of the Board of Education in Massachusetts, fought for higher teacher qualifications, better pay, newer school buildings, and an improved curriculum.

For the first time, women also gained access to higher learning during the antebellum period. Feminist Mary Lyon, for example, established the all-women's Mount Holyoke Seminary in 1837, while progressive Oberlin College began admitting women the same year.

CHAPTER 7
1820–1860

THE WOMEN'S SUFFRAGE MOVEMENT

Women reformers also fought for gender equality. In the years before the Civil War, many Americans continued to believe that men and women worked in separate spheres: men outside the home, and women inside. Sometimes referred to as the "cult of domesticity," this social norm encouraged "good" women to make the home a happy and nurturing environment for their wage-laborer husbands, on top of maintaining day-to-day housekeeping.

The Seneca Falls Convention

As the American economy changed and more women left the sphere of the home for the workforce, many women began demanding more social, political, and economic rights. Prominent leaders of the women's rights movement included Lucretia Mott and **Elizabeth Cady Stanton**. These women astounded Americans and Europeans alike when they met at the **Seneca Falls Convention** in Seneca Falls, New York, in 1848. There, women leaders drafted a **Declaration of Sentiments** in the spirit of the Declaration of Independence to declare that women were equal to men in every way. Of the many sentiments declared, the call for full political suffrage shocked the world the most.

The American Renaissance

The early nineteenth century gave rise to **Romanticism**, a cultural movement in Europe and America that revolted against the certainty and rationalism of the Enlightenment. In America, Romanticism manifested itself as a literary and artistic awakening in thought, literature, and the arts. Americans took great interest in the movement, idealizing its emphasis on the individual and the common man. Romanticism underscored feeling and emotion, in contrast with the balance, harmony, and form of eighteenth-century Classicism.

THE ROMANTICS

Romantics, such as John Greenleaf Whittier, Louisa May Alcott, and Henry Wadsworth Longfellow, tried to capture their thoughts and emotions as well as the spirit of the new America. Other social commentators included the so-called **Dark Romantics**, such as Edgar Allan Poe, Herman Melville, and Nathaniel Hawthorne, who took a more critical view of American society in the years before the Civil War.

THE TRANSCENDENTALISTS

The New England **Transcendentalists** argued that not all knowledge comes from the senses and that ultimate truth "transcends" the physical world. Transcendentalists believed in the divinity of man's inner consciousness and thought that nature revealed the whole of God's moral law. Between 1830 and 1850, Transcendentalists like **Ralph Waldo Emerson**, Henry David Thoreau, and Walt Whitman championed self-reliance and a rugged individuality that matched the character of the developing nation.

AMERICAN ART

For the first time, American painting was reaching a level comparable to that of contemporary European artists. American artists worked within the Romantic Movement and sought to create unique aesthetic forms. Folk art attained popularity as did landscape paintings by the **Luminists** and **Hudson River School**. Americans also liked **Currier and Ives** lithographs, which portrayed rural and domestic scenes.

The blossoming artistic scene, however, belied a growing unease throughout the country. The slavery issue in particular began to occupy center stage in American politics, especially as new western states petitioned to join the Union. The disputes escalated into sporadic violence in the 1850s, pushing the North and South closer and closer to civil war.

CHAPTER 7
1820–1860

How did the Market Revolution affect the United States socially, politically, and economically?

The Market Revolution had a variety of economic, social, and political effects on the United States. The most important results emerged from the development of industrial machines such as the cotton gin. The use of these machines gave rise to the trade of manufactured goods, which created greater economic interdependency between the major geographic regions of the country. This in turn produced new social classes, whose members pursued conflicting political goals. In combination, these developments pushed the North and South further apart, setting the stage for the Civil War.

Economically, the Market Revolution set America on a course for full-scale industrial revolution. Automated machines such as the cotton gin and the mower-reaper transformed the previously low-volume, labor-intensive crops of cotton and wheat into massively profitable, high-volume cash crops. In the South, plantation owners abandoned their other crops in order to move to full-time cotton production, which quickly became the basis of the southern economy. The South's new cotton industry caused a textile boom in the North, and cloth factories appeared throughout the middle states and New England. While these developments were outwardly positive, they would ultimately create greater tension between the North and South.

Socially, the effects of the Market Revolution greatly contributed to the development of new classes in all parts of the country. In the South, the new cotton industry produced a group of ultra-rich and very influential plantation owners. These new cotton barons were dependant upon the institution of slavery. While slavery had a long tradition in the South, it had never been such a fundamental part of the region's economic survival. The size of individual plantations increased from relatively small farms to huge operations that depended upon the labor of hundreds of slaves. Meanwhile, in the North, the rapidly growing textile industry gave rise to both the wage-labor system and urbanization. Consequently, it also resulted in a much larger and

Student Essay

richer merchant class with an increasingly ambitious political agenda.

The political effects of the Market Revolution were of no less importance than the social and economic effects. In particular, the new class of wealthy merchants in the North led to the formation of the nationalistic Whig party. The Whigs sought higher protective tariffs, more internal improvements, and a Central Bank of the United States. However, greater centralization in the government did not sit well in the South, which was just beginning to feel more independent due to its newfound economic strength. Additionally, with the South's dependence on slavery, tension over the issue grew with the North, which generally frowned upon the practice and sought to restrict or even ban it. Over time, the slavery issue became increasingly contentious. Despite the North's dependence on the South to supply its growing textile industry with cotton, it failed to recognize that without slavery, this supply would likely disappear. The South naturally felt threatened that the North was going to destroy its way of life. It is hardly surprising that slavery became a fundamental part of the platforms of many southern politicians, and in turn resulted in political conflict between the North and South.

During the Market Revolution, the relationship between North and South became increasingly complex as various economic, social, and political effects all came into play. The South's expanding cotton industry affected both the North and the South on an economic level. New social classes emerged in both regions as a result, and these groups soon had their own political agendas, putting them in direct opposition to one another. These divergent economic, social, and political paths would pull the North and the South further and further apart. When the debate over slavery turned violent, politicians representing the two sections of the country began to wonder if they could ever learn to work together. Soon, the secession of several southern states would lead the nation to ponder this question as well.

Test Questions and Answers

1. What factors contributed to the Market Revolution in the United States?

- Americans employed newly invented technologies.
- Immigration helped northern industries grow.
- New markets opened because of internal transportation improvements like canals and trains.

2. What social issues did antebellum reformers tackle?

- Prisons and insane asylums
- Public education
- The rights of women
- Slavery
- Prostitution
- Alcoholism

3. What characteristics did most antebellum reformers share?

- Most were northerners.
- Most were women.
- Most had been affected by Great Awakening revivalism.

4. How did antebellum northern society differ from antebellum southern society?

- Society in the South was extremely hierarchical.
- Irish and German immigrants poured into northern industrial cities.
- Northerners were much more involved in the reform movement than southerners.
- Wage labor in the North contrasted sharply with slavery in the South.

5. *How did the Market Revolution affect the North, West, and South?*

- Cyrus McCormick's mechanical mower-reaper allowed western farmers to grow large grain surpluses to feed the exploding populations in the Northeast.

- Eli Whitney's cotton gin allowed southern planters to grow cotton to sell to English and northeastern textile factories.

- Northeastern textile factories produced goods to ship to the farmers and planters in the West and South.

- Internal improvements such as canals and roads plus new inventions like railroads and steamboats made shipping these goods fast and cost-efficient.

Timeline

1793	Eli Whitney invents the cotton gin.
1798	Whitney invents interchangeable parts for firearms.
1800	The Second Great Awakening begins.
1807	Robert Fulton invents the steamboat.
1823	Lowell Mills opens in Waltham, Massachusetts.
1825	The Erie Canal is completed.
	The New Harmony commune is founded.
1826	The American Temperance Society is founded.
1828	The first American railroad is completed.
1830	The Transcendentalist movement begins.
	Joseph Smith establishes the Mormon Church.
	Charles Grandison Finney begins conducting Christian revivals.
1831	Nat Turner leads a slave rebellion in Virginia.
	William Lloyd Garrison begins publishing *The Liberator*.
1833	The National Trades Union forms.
	Garrison and Theodore Weld found the American Anti-Slavery Society.
1834	Cyrus McCormick invents the mechanical mower-reaper.
1836	The House of Representatives passes the "Gag Resolution."
1837	John Deere invents the steel plow.
	Oberlin College begins admitting women.
	Mary Lyon establishes Mount Holyoke Seminary.
1840	Van Buren establishes a ten-hour working day for federal employees.
1841	The Brook Farm commune is founded.
1843	Dorothea Dix crusades for prison and insane asylum reform.
	Millerites prepare for the end of the world.
1846	Mormons begin migration to Utah.

1848	The Seneca Falls Women's Rights Convention is held.
	The Oneida Community is founded.
1850	Nathaniel Hawthorne publishes *The Scarlet Letter*.
1851	Herman Melville publishes *Moby-Dick*.
1852	The Cumberland Road is completed .
1854	Henry David Thoreau writes *Walden*.
	T. S. Arthur publishes the novel *Ten Nights in a Barroom and What I Saw There*.
1855	Walt Whitman publishes *Leaves of Grass*.

Major Figures

Dorothea Dix A schoolteacher from Massachusetts, Dix spearheaded the campaign to establish publicly funded insane asylums to help the mentally ill. Her report on the deplorable treatment of insane women in the state's prisons convinced legislators to build the first asylums. Dix traveled tens of thousands of miles promoting her cause.

Ralph Waldo Emerson One of America's leading essayists and philosophers, Emerson was also one of the foremost Transcendentalists in the 1830s, 1840s, and 1850s. His essays—including the famous *Self-Reliance*—made him one of the nation's most popular practical philosophers.

Charles Grandison Finney A former lawyer, Finney applied his sharp wits and keen intellect to preach evangelism throughout the North during the 1830s. His camp-style meetings put thousands of people into a frenzy during his fifty-year crusade. He encouraged women to become church leaders and railed against the evils of slavery and alcohol.

William Lloyd Garrison A radical abolitionist, Garrison advocated the immediate emancipation of all slaves in the United States. His infamous magazine *The Liberator* earned him many enemies in the South.

Horace Mann A champion of public education, Mann supervised the creation of many new tax-supported schools as the secretary of the Massachusetts Board of Education in the 1830s. He fought for better curriculum, higher pay for teachers, and more teacher qualifications.

Joseph Smith A New Yorker from the Burned-Over District, Smith founded the Mormon Church (Church of Jesus Christ of Latter Day Saints) after claiming to have received a new set of gospels from an angel. Smith attracted a huge following but was forced to move to the Midwest to escape persecution for his belief in polygamy. After he was murdered by a mob, his disciple Brigham Young led thousands of Mormons to the Great Salt Lake in Utah. The Mormon Church was one of the more successful new religions to sprout from the Burned-Over District.

Elizabeth Cady Stanton One of the first American feminists, Stanton called for social and political equality for women in the nineteenth century. She helped organize the Seneca Falls Convention in 1848 and drafted the Declaration of Sentiments.

Eli Whitney Inventor of the cotton gin and interchangeable parts, Whitney completely changed the American economy and social fabric. His 1793 cotton gin made growing cotton easy and highly profitable for southern planters, who eventually converted most of their fields to growing the crop. The surge in production also required more black slaves to pick the cotton. Southern cotton and interchangeable parts in turn stimulated the growth of textile manufacturing in the North and the birth of the wage labor system.

Suggested Reading

- Larkin, Jack. *The Reshaping of Everyday Life: 1790-1840.* New York: Perennial, 1989.

Larkin's book focuses on the social change that evolved throughout roughly the first five decades of life in the United States.

- Mintz, Steven. *Moralists and Modernizers: America's Pre-Civil War Reformers.* Baltimore: Johns Hopkins University Press, 1995.

While the era spanning the revolution to the Civil War is not known for its social and political reforms, Mintz's work highlights the major contributions of individuals in this era to reform movements in the post–Civil War era.

- Sellers, Charles. *The Market Revolution: Jacksonian America 1815-1846.* New York: Oxford University Press, 1994.

The book details Jackson's profound impact on the developing economy of the young United States.

- Wilentz, Sean. *Chants Democratic: New York City and the Rise of the American Working Class, 1788-1850.* New York: Oxford University Press, 1986.

Wilentz's book is an examination of the American worker from the revolution to the Civil War through the lens of politics and culture in New York City.

Prelude to War: 1848–1859

8

- Slavery and Expansion
- The Kansas–Nebraska Crisis
- Prelude to War

Some historians call the Mexican War the first battle of the Civil War, because it ignited an intense debate within America over the westward expansion of slavery. Most northerners generally opposed slavery in the Mexican Cession (the territory comprising present-day California, Arizona, New Mexico, Nevada, Colorado, Utah, and Wyoming), while southerners thought the expansion of slavery necessary in order to maintain their social and economic way of life.

By 1857, disputes over slavery had become so bitter and violent that peaceful resolution seemed impossible. The Compromise of 1850 had only served to preserve the peace for a few short years, and historians now view it as proof of the inability of the statesmen involved to forcefully address an issue that threatened to destroy their way of life. The events in Kansas during the 1850s, in which pro- and antislavery forces fought bloody battles to determine whether Kansas would become a free or a slave state, as well as the caning of Charles Sumner, an antislavery senator from Massachusetts, show the extent to which the debate had unraveled. As a result, it only took a little nudging to bring the North and South to the brink of war. The Lincoln–Douglas debates in 1858 captured the nation's attention, and while by all accounts Lincoln lost the debates, he was thrust into the public spotlight. Lincoln would return to the debate floor in 1860 as the presidential candidate for the Republican party.

Slavery and Expansion

The new lands west of Texas that had been yielded to the United States at the end of the Mexican War rekindled the debate over the westward expansion of slavery. Southern politicians and slave owners wanted to permit slavery in the West out of fear that a ban would spell doom for the institution, as the South would lose the newly created seats in Congress. Whig northerners, however, viewed slavery as a moral evil and wanted it banned. Tensions mounted when Pennsylvanian congressman David Wilmot proposed banning slavery in the territory in the **Wilmot Proviso** in 1846, even before the Mexican War had ended. Outraged, southerners immediately killed the proposition in the Senate.

THE ELECTION OF 1848

The debate over the westward expansion of slavery dominated the election of 1848 despite the death of the Wilmot Proviso, which would prohibit slavery in the western territories. Three major candidates contended for the presidency that year:

- **Lewis Cass**, on the Democratic ticket. Cass championed **popular sovereignty**, which would allow people in the western territories to decide for themselves whether to legalize slavery in their state

- **Zachary Taylor**, the Whig candidate, a Mexican–American War hero who chose not to address the slavery issue

- **Martin Van Buren,** the **Free Soil Party** candidate, who ran on an abolitionist platform

Van Buren's entry into the race split the Democrats and allowed Zachary Taylor to win easily. Although Taylor's silence on the slavery question quelled further discussion for a time, the issue resurfaced less than a year later when California applied for statehood. As a result, a great debate quickly divided northerners and southerners in Congress over the future of slavery beyond the Mississippi.

THE COMPROMISE OF 1850

In 1850, the North and South once again agreed to compromise on the issue of slavery and California's acceptance into the

California's population exploded in 1849 when tens of thousands of Americans dashed out West in the **Gold Rush** hoping to strike it rich. These fortune hunters were called "'49ers" for the year they left home. While thousands moved west, few struck it as rich as they had dreamed.

Union. Although **Henry Clay** deserves most of the credit for engineering the compromise, a younger generation of politicians, like Illinois senator **Stephen Douglas**, hammered out most of the details of the **Compromise of 1850**:

- California entered the Union as a free state.

- Northerners and southerners agreed that popular sovereignty would determine the fate of slavery in all other western territories.

- Texas gave up territorial claims west of the Rio Grande (in New Mexico) in return for $10 million.

- Washington, D.C., abolished the slave trade but not slavery itself.

- Congress passed a new and stronger **Fugitive Slave Law**, which required northerners to return runaway slaves to southern plantation owners.

Although President Taylor opposed the compromise, he unexpectedly died most likely from cholera in 1850 before he could veto it. Instead, Vice President **Millard Fillmore** became president and signed the compromise into law in September 1850.

Significance of the Compromise

The Compromise of 1850 benefited the North far more than the South:

- California's admission tipped the precious sectional balance in the Senate in favor of the North with sixteen free states to fifteen slave states.

- California's admission to the Union as a free state set a precedent in the West against the expansion of slavery.

- Southerners conceded to end the slave trade in Washington, D.C.

- The compromise averted civil war for ten more years, allowing the North to develop industrially.

Though the compromise granted Californians popular sovereignty, meaning they were allowed to decide for themselves whether to allow slavery, northerners knew that slavery would never take root in the West. Cotton couldn't grow in the arid western climate, and therefore the need for slaves would not be as great as it was in the South.

> Even though the agreement clearly favored northerners, southerners were willing to make so many concessions because they truly believed the Compromise of 1850 would end the debate over slavery. This belief turned out to be very far from the truth.

Northern Reaction to the Fugitive Slave Law

The new Fugitive Slave Law only fanned the abolitionist flame instead of relieving sectional tensions. Even though most white Americans in the North harbored no love for blacks, they didn't want to re-enslave those who had escaped to freedom. Consequently, armed mobs of northerners sometimes attacked slave catchers to free captured slaves. On one occasion, it took several hundred troops and a naval ship to escort a single captured slave through the streets of Boston and back to the South to prevent mobs from freeing him. The law helped transform abolitionism from a radical philosophy into a mainstream movement in the North.

The Underground Railroad

Even though very few slaves actually escaped to the North, the mere fact that northern abolitionists encouraged slaves to run away infuriated southern plantation owners. Despite this fury, there were those in the South who helped slaves escape to freedom. The **Underground Railroad** successfully ferried as many as several thousand fugitive slaves into the North and into Canada during these years. "Conductor" **Harriet Tubman** supposedly delivered several hundred slaves to freedom herself.

Harriet Beecher Stowe's 1852 novel *Uncle Tom's Cabin* also had a profound effect on northerners. Stowe sold hundreds of thousands of copies within just a few months and turned many northerners against slavery.

> *Harriet Beecher Stowe's* Uncle Tom's Cabin *turned northern public opinion against slavery and the South so much that when Abraham Lincoln met Stowe in 1863, he commented, "So you're the little woman who wrote the book that made this great war!"*

PIERCE AND EXPANSION IN 1852

After the Compromise of 1850, southerners quickly sought out new territories to expand the cotton kingdom. The election of **Franklin Pierce** to the presidency in 1852 only helped their cause. Pierce was a pro-South Democrat from New England and a firm believer in Manifest Destiny who also hoped to expand the United States.

Walker in Nicaragua

Pierce became particularly interested in acquiring new territories in Latin America during his presidency. He even went so far as to quietly support a coup in Nicaragua led by southern adventurer **William Walker**, who hoped that Pierce would annex Nicaragua as Polk had annexed Texas in 1844. The plan failed, however, when several other Latin American countries sent troops to remove Walker from power.

Cuba, Japan, and the Gadsden Purchase

Pierce also threatened to steal Cuba from Spain in a letter called the **Ostend Manifesto**. His plans failed when northern journalists received a leaked copy of the letter and published it in 1854. Despite these failures, Pierce did acquire 30,000 square miles of New Mexican territory from Mexico in the **Gadsden Purchase** in 1853 and successfully opened Japan to American trade later that year.

The Kansas-Nebraska Crisis

To prevent railroad developers from building a transcontinental railroad through the South and Southwest, which would aid the spread of slavery, Illinois senator **Stephen Douglas** proposed instead to build the line farther north through the vast unorganized territory west of the Mississippi River. Douglas proposed the **Kansas–Nebraska Act** in 1854 to create two new territories, Kansas and Nebraska, North of the 36° 30' parallel, as the law stipulated that developers could only lay railroad tracks in states or in federal territories. Because Douglas knew that southerners would never approve two new free territories, he instead declared that **popular sovereignty** would determine whether Kansas and Nebraska would enter the Union as free or slave states.

Kansas-Nebraska Act

Douglas made an enormous error in proposing the Kansas–Nebraska Act. Southern Democrats and Whigs alike jumped at the opportunity to open northern territories to slavery and quickly passed the act. Northerners, however, felt outraged that Douglas and the southerners had effectively revoked the sacred Missouri Compromise of 1820, which banned slavery north of the 36° 30' parallel. Hundreds of riots and protests consequently erupted in northern cities, and many people began to feel that differences between the North and South had become irreconcilable.

> The Kansas–Nebraska Act split both the Whig and Democratic parties into sectional factions as southern Whigs voted with the southern Democrats against their northern counterparts to pass the act through Congress. The Whig party never recovered from the split.

BLEEDING KANSAS

As soon as Congress passed the Kansas–Nebraska Act, thousands of proslavery Missourians crossed the state line into Kansas and claimed as much land as they could. Hoping to make Kansas another slave territory, these **"Border Ruffians"** also rigged elections and recruited friends and family in Missouri to cast illegal ballots. Others voted multiple times or threatened indifferent settlers to vote in favor of slavery. Shocked, northern abolitionists flocked to the state to establish their own free-soil towns.

The Pottawatomie Massacre

Violence eventually erupted when a group of Border Ruffians burned the free-soil (antislavery) town of Lawrence. In retaliation, a deranged abolitionist named **John Brown**, along with his own band of men, butchered five proslavery settlers in the **Pottawatomie Massacre**. No court ever punished Brown or his followers. Within a few months, Border Ruffians and free-soilers in **"Bleeding Kansas"** had become embroiled in a bloody civil war that foreshadowed the looming greater Civil War.

The Caning of Charles Sumner

The crisis in Kansas deeply shocked and divided Americans, as evidenced by the caning of Massachusetts senator **Charles Sumner** on the Senate floor. Incensed over an antislavery speech Sumner had delivered after violence erupted in Kansas, Congressman Preston Brooks from South Carolina mercilessly beat Sumner with his cane on the floor of the Senate. The beating nearly killed the Massachusetts senator, who ultimately left the Senate for several years to receive medical treatment. Southerners hailed Brooks as a hero, while northerners called him a barbarian. Violence on the floor of the Senate, and the vastly differing reactions to the violence, were more indicators that pro- and antislavery factions had moved beyond debate.

THE ELECTION OF 1856

Bleeding Kansas dominated the election of 1856, and parties nominated Kansas-neutral candidates in the hope of avoiding sectionalism. The Whig Party had by this time completely dissolved over the slavery and popular sovereignty question, and former Whigs in the North chose to unite with the Free-Soil Party and unionist Democrats to form the new **Republican Party**. There were three candidates for president in 1856:

- **John C. Frémont**, the new Republican-nominated adventurer, on a platform against the westward expansion of slavery.

- **James Buchanan**, the Democrat-nominated and relatively unknown who championed popular sovereignty (allowing states to decide for themselves whether to enter the Union as slave or free).

- **Millard Fillmore**, ex-president of the nativist **Know-Nothing Party**, on an anti-immigration platform.

Because most southern state legislatures threatened to secede from the Union if Frémont became president, Buchanan won easily. Many northerners, shocked by the violence in Kansas and unprepared for a larger civil war, ultimately voted for the Democrat in order to keep the Union intact, whether they agreed with popular sovereignty or not.

The South's political victory with Buchanan in 1856 actually helped ensure the North's military victory in the Civil War, as it gave the North more time to develop its manufacturing capabilities. The North's ability to manufacture guns, cannons, and other supplies proved vital to the Union victory and also highlighted the economic differences with the South, which had abundant resources but no way to manufacture the items that it needed.

THE LECOMPTON CONSTITUTION

Because abolitionist settlers and Border Ruffians couldn't agree on a territorial government in Kansas, they each established their own. The free-soil legislature resided in Topeka, and the proslavery government in Lecompton. After free-soilers boycotted a rigged election to choose delegates to draft a state constitution in 1857, proslavery settlers decided to write their own. After drafting the **Lecompton Constitution**, which permitted slavery and placed no restrictions on the importation of slaves into the territory, they then applied for statehood as a slave state.

President Buchanan immediately accepted the constitution and welcomed Kansas into the Union. The Republican-dominated Congress, however, refused to admit Kansas. Senator Douglas declared that Congress would only admit Kansas after honest elections had determined whether the state would be free or slave. The following year, an overwhelming number of Kansas voters flatly rejected the Lecompton Constitution in a referendum, and Kansas entered the Union as a free state in 1861.

Bleeding Kansas and the Lecompton Constitution revealed the inherent weakness of the idea of Popular Sovereignty, in which a popular vote would decide the slavery issue. The issue of slavery had become so charged with emotion that certifiable elections were almost impossible, as both sides seem willing to intimidate voters and illegally affect the outcome of elections.

Prelude to War

North-South relations worsened throughout Buchanan's four years in office. By 1859, civil war appeared inevitable.

THE DRED SCOTT CASE

In the 1840s, a Missouri slave named **Dred Scott** sued his master for his family's freedom on the grounds that they had lived with his master for several years in the free states north of the 36° 30' parallel. In fact, his wife and daughter had been born in the North but had become slaves as soon as they accompanied Scott back into the South. In 1857, the case landed in the Supreme Court, where Chief Justice Roger Taney and other conservative justices ruled that only citizens, not slaves, could file lawsuits in federal courts. Moreover, Taney declared the Missouri Compromise of 1820 unconstitutional because the government could not restrict the movement of private property.

Essentially, Taney and the Court argued that slaves had no legal rights because they were property. Taney hoped that the **Dred Scott Decision** in *Dred Scott v. Sanford* would permanently end the sectional debate over slavery.

Northern Backlash to Dred Scott

Instead, the Dred Scott ruling only exacerbated sectional tensions. Southerners praised the ruling while northerners recoiled in horror. Thousands took to the streets in the North to protest the decision, and many questioned the impartiality of the southern-dominated Supreme Court. Several state legislatures even nullified the decision and declared that their states would never permit slavery, no matter who ordered them to do so. Many also accused James Buchanan of bias when journalists uncovered that the president had pressured a northern Supreme Court justice into siding with Taney and the southerners.

THE LINCOLN-DOUGLAS DEBATES

In this atmosphere of national confusion, a relatively unknown former congressman named **Abraham Lincoln** challenged Stephen Douglas to a series of public debates in their home state of Illinois. Lincoln hoped to steal Douglas's seat in the Senate in the 1858 elections and to be the first to put the question of slavery to the voters. Douglas accepted Lincoln's offer and engaged Lincoln in a total of seven public debates in front of several thousand people. Lincoln denounced slavery as a moral wrong and voiced his desire to see the "peculiar institution" banned entirely in the West. At the same time, however, he also expressed his deep desire to preserve the Union.

Douglas, meanwhile, called Lincoln a radical abolitionist and argued in the **Freeport Doctrine** that only popular sovereignty would provide a democratic solution to resolving the slavery debate in the West. Even though Lincoln lost the Senate seat, the **Lincoln–Douglas Debates** made Lincoln a national figure.

JOHN BROWN'S RAID

On October 16, 1859, John Brown of Pottawatomie, Kansas, stormed an arsenal at **Harpers Ferry**, Virginia, with twenty other men hoping to spark a slave rebellion in Virginia and throughout the South. Strangely, the insane Brown had forgotten to inform any slaves of his intentions, and therefore no slaves rose up against their masters. Instead, Brown and his men found themselves trapped inside the arsenal and surrounded by federal troops. Brown eventually surrendered after a long and bloody standoff that killed more than half his men, including his own son.

After a speedy trial, a federal court convicted and hanged Brown. Before his death, the unwavering Brown dramatically announced that he'd gladly die if his death brought the nation closer to justice.

Reactions North and South

Southerners applauded Brown's execution, because his raid on Harpers Ferry had touched on the southerners' deepest fear: that the slaves would one day rise up against them. To them, Brown had been a criminal and a traitor of the worst kind. Northerners, however, mourned his death because they considered him an abolitionist martyr, especially after so boldly denouncing slavery with his final words. He instantly became a national hero and patriot, despite the fact that he'd clearly broken the law. The northerners' reaction shocked southerners, driving the two groups further apart.

CHAPTER 8
1848–1859

Was the Civil War inevitable?

The Civil War was indeed inevitable. During the early nineteenth
century, the North and South followed vastly different economic
and cultural paths, the central pillar of this divergence being the
rapid expansion of the southern cotton industry. By the election of
1860, these fundamentally different ways of life were reflected in
the political leaders of the country. When these conflicting ideals
became the main political themes, argued by men who felt their
way of life was at stake, there was no option available other than
war.

The sudden expansion of the cotton industry during the early
1800s completely transformed the southern economy, giving the
region a new source of wealth and independence. Eli Whitney's
invention of the cotton gin in 1793 changed cotton into a
massively profitable cash crop. By separating cottonseeds from
usable cotton, the machine was capable of doing in minutes what
human laborers required hours to do by hand. Soon, many
plantation owners abandoned almost all other crops in order to
concentrate on the lucrative new cotton trade. Small farmers
switched to producing cotton as well, but the economic power lay
in the hands of the large plantation owners.

While the cotton gin greatly accelerated the processing of
cotton, human labor remained a fundamental part of the planting
and harvesting process. In order to raise more cotton, plantation
owners purchased large numbers of slaves from Africa and the
West Indies and brought thousands of them into the country to
tend the cotton fields. The size of plantations swelled from
relatively small farms to huge operations that in some cases used
hundreds of slaves. The entire southern economy depended on
cotton and therefore depended on slavery. During the 1850s, the
North's position on slavery strengthened as public opinion turned
more adamantly against it. Works like *Uncle Tom's Cabin* by
Harriet Beecher Stowe awakened northerners to the plight of
southern slaves. Worse, events such as the "Bleeding Kansas"
debacle, in which violent battles broke out over whether slavery

would be allowed in new territories, forced many people to take firm sides on the issue.

Cotton transformed southern society and politics as well. Wealthy plantation owners emerged as the central feature of the social scene, and as in most agrarian societies, land equaled power. With most plantations as big as small villages, and with the majority of the population spread out over the countryside, personal freedom and liberties took precedence over social equality and reform. Soon, large plantation owners had the ears—and minds—of the political leaders from the South. Most of these leaders were Democrats by the election of 1860, and more and more often, political parties were drawn along sectional lines. Increasingly wary of what they perceived to be northern efforts to control their way of life, politicians representing the South in Congress and in the Senate were unwilling to amend their beliefs.

Northern states developed in a completely different direction. Where southerners moved to the rural countryside, northerners concentrated in cities. Where the South was based on an agrarian economy, northern states turned to industry, specifically to textile mills and factories that needed the cotton that the South was harvesting. Despite this reliance on southern cotton, northerners also grew increasingly concerned about the institution of slavery, not only as it existed in the South, but whether it would exist in the new midwestern and western territories. Additionally, as the election of 1860 approached, social equality and reform formed the basis of a major movement in northern cities, a movement that was almost nonexistent south of the Mason–Dixon line. Northerners began to look on the South as stuck in the past, in a less modern time, and in a way of life that was morally wrong. When northern political leaders began voicing these opinions, southerners became determined to protect their way of life. There seemed little room for compromise.

Too much was at stake for either the North or the South to give in to the other, and much stood in the balance with the election of 1860. The Democrats eventually nominated Stephen Douglas after many party members in the South had abandoned the convention to nominate their own "states' rights" candidate. The Republicans nominated a little-known politician from Illinois named Abraham Lincoln, who ran on a platform that promised to halt the expansion of slavery. The result was a landslide victory for the Republicans. Southerners feared northern attempts to change their way of life and each state's right to govern its own citizens, and northerners felt it was only a matter of time before they would have to pull the South away from an anachronistic culture. With Lincoln now in the White House, southerners felt they had no alternative but secession, which the North and Lincoln were unwilling to accept.

Test Questions and Answers

1. Why did so many yeoman farmers support slavery when so few of them actually owned slaves?

- Almost all southerners hoped to own slaves one day.

- All southerners enjoyed the by-products of slavery, such as a healthy economy.

- Most white southerners enjoyed the benefits of their racially superior position.

2. How did slaves attempt to resist bondage?

- Many worked slowly, had low productivity standards, or feigned illness.

- Some slaves ran away or, like Nat Turner, staged revolts.

3. Why did popular sovereignty fail to resolve the debate over permitting slavery in the new western territories?

- A significant minority of northerners were unwilling to compromise and wanted immediate abolition.

- Northerners feared that slavery could one day spread into the North.

- Popular sovereignty had led to civil war in "Bleeding Kansas."

4. Why did so few northerners embrace the abolitionist movement?

- Radical abolitionists advocated equal rights for blacks.

- Though most northerners believed that slavery was morally wrong, few believed that African Americans were socially, intellectually, or legally equal to whites.

5. What was the impact of the Compromise of 1850?

- Northerners hated the stronger Fugitive Slave Law.

- The compromise postponed the Civil War for ten years, which ultimately gave the industrialized and more populous North a distinct advantage.

- The compromise tipped the sectional balance in the Senate in favor of the North: sixteen free states to fifteen slave states.

Timeline

1846	David Wilmot proposes the Wilmot Proviso.
1848	The Mexican War ends.
	The Free Soil Party forms.
	Zachary Taylor is elected president.
1849	California petitions for admission to the Union.
1850	The Compromise of 1850 includes the passage of the Fugitive Slave Law.
	Taylor dies from cholera.
	Millard Fillmore becomes president.
1852	Franklin Pierce is elected president.
	Harriet Beecher Stowe publishes *Uncle Tom's Cabin*.
1854	Pierce threatens to acquire Cuba in the Ostend Manifesto.
	Stephen Douglas proposes the Kansas–Nebraska Act.
	The Republican Party forms.
1855	William Walker takes Nicaragua.
1856	The Bleeding Kansas crisis shocks northern abolitionists.
	The Pottawatomie Massacre foreshadows the Civil War.
	Charles Sumner is attacked in the Senate.
	James Buchanan is elected president.
1857	Buchanan accepts the Lecompton Constitution.
	The Supreme Court issues its Dred Scott decision.
	The Panic of 1857 hits.
1858	Congress rejects the Lecompton Constitution.
	Abraham Lincoln and Stephen Douglas debate slavery in Illinois.
1859	John Brown raids Harpers Ferry.

Major Figures

John Brown Undoubtedly certifiably insane, Brown was a zealous radical abolitionist from Ohio who violently crusaded against slavery in the 1850s. He moved to Kansas in the mid-1850s with his family to prevent the territory from becoming a slave state. In 1856, he and a band of vigilantes helped spark the Bleeding Kansas crisis when they slaughtered five Border Ruffians at the Pottawatomie Massacre. Three years later, Brown led another group of men in the Harpers Ferry Raid to incite a slave rebellion. He was captured during the raid and hanged shortly before the election of 1860. Though Brown's death was cheered in the South, he was mourned in the North.

James Buchanan A pro-South Democrat, Buchanan became the fifteenth president of the United States in 1856 after defeating John Frémont of the new Republican party and former president Millard Fillmore of the Know-Nothing party in one of the most hotly contested elections in U.S. history. Buchanan supported the Lecompton Constitution to admit Kansas as a slave state, weathered the Panic of 1857, and did nothing to prevent South Carolina's secession from the Union.

Lewis Cass As Democratic candidate for the presidency against Zachary Taylor and Martin Van Buren in 1848, Cass was the first to propose allowing Americans in the territories to choose for themselves whether to be free or slave states. The doctrine of popular sovereignty was the hottest election topic in the years leading up to the Civil War.

John C. Calhoun Even though Calhoun served as vice president to both John Quincy Adams and Andrew Jackson, he also led the movement to nullify the 1828 Tariff of Abominations in South Carolina. Shortly after Congress passed the tariff, he wrote *The South Carolina Exposition* that urged South Carolina legislators to declare the tax null and void in the state. *The Exposition* and Nullification Crisis brought about the greatest challenge the nation had yet faced and illustrated the emerging sectional differences. Calhoun is also regarded as one of America's finest political theorists.

Henry Clay Also known as the Great Pacificator, this Kentuckian served as speaker of the House of Representatives, secretary of state to John Quincy Adams, and later as a U.S. senator. He was the father of the American System to promote higher tariffs and internal improvements at government expense. Clay earned his nickname for devising both the Missouri Compromise of 1820 and the compromise Tariff of 1833 to end the nullification crisis. In 1834, he allied himself with Daniel Webster of New England to form the Whigs, a progressive new political party for internal improvements, limited westward expansion, and reform. He also engineered the Compromise of 1850, which ultimately postponed the inevitable clash between the North and the South. Even though he never served as president (he ran and lost four times), historians regard him as one of America's greatest statesmen.

Stephen Douglas A Democratic senator from Illinois, Douglas pushed the Kansas–Nebraska Act through Congress in 1854 to entice railroad developers to build a transcontinental railroad line in the North. The act opened Kansas and Nebraska territories to slavery and thus effectively repealed the Missouri Compromise of 1820. Douglas rejected the proslavery Lecompton Constitution in the Senate in 1857 after Border Ruffians had rigged the elections to draft a state constitution. A champion of popular sovereignty, he announced his Freeport Doctrine in response to the Dred Scott decision in the Lincoln–Douglas debates against Abraham Lincoln in 1858. Although he was the most popular Democrat, southern party members refused to nominate him for the presidency in 1860 because he had rejected the Lecompton Constitution to make Kansas a slave state. As a result, the party split: northern Democrats nominated Douglas, while southern Democrats nominated John C. Breckinridge. In the election of 1860, Douglas toured the country in an effort to save the Union.

Millard Fillmore Vice President Fillmore became the thirteenth president when Zachary Taylor died two years into his term in 1850. He served unremarkably for the remainder of Taylor's term. He later ran on the Know-Nothing party ticket against James Buchanan and John C. Frémont in 1856.

Abraham Lincoln A former lawyer from Illinois, Lincoln became the sixteenth president of the United States in the election of 1860. Because he was a Republican and associated with the abolitionist cause, his election prompted South Carolina to become the first state to secede from the Union. Lincoln believed that the states had legally never truly left the Union, but fought the war until the South surrendered unconditionally. He proposed the Ten-Percent Plan for Reconstruction in 1863, but was assassinated by John Wilkes Booth before he could carry out his plans.

Franklin Pierce Elected in 1852, Pierce was a proslavery Democrat from New England. He combined his desire for empire and westward expansion with the South's desire to find new slave territories. He tacitly backed William

Walker's attempt to seize Nicaragua, and threatened Spain in the Ostend Manifesto for Cuba. He also sent Commodore Matthew Perry to forcibly pry open Japan to American trade, and authorized the Gadsden Purchase from Mexico in 1853. Pierce's reputation was muddied by his alliance with the South, his aggressive expansionism, and by Bleeding Kansas.

Dred Scott A slave to a southern army doctor, Scott had lived with his master in Illinois and the Wisconsin territory in the 1830s. While there, he married a free woman and had a daughter who eventually went back with Scott to the South. Scott sued his master for his and his family's freedom, but Chief Justice Roger Taney and a conservative Supreme Court ruled against Scott, arguing that Congress had no right to restrict the movement of private property. Moreover, he ruled that blacks like Scott could not file lawsuits in federal courts because they were not citizens. The Dred Scott decision outraged northerners and drove them further from the South.

Charles Sumner In 1856, Senator Sumner from Massachusetts delivered an antislavery speech in the wake of the Bleeding Kansas crisis. In response, he was nearly caned to death by South Carolinian congressman Preston Brooks on the Senate floor. The caning demonstrated just how seriously southerners took the popular sovereignty and slavery issue.

Zachary Taylor A hero of the Mexican War, Taylor became the second and last Whig president in 1848. He campaigned without a solid platform to avoid controversy over the westward expansion of slavery in the Mexican Cession. He died after only two years in office and was replaced by Millard Fillmore.

Harriet Tubman An illiterate runaway slave from Maryland, Tubman was an active abolitionist as one of the key "conductors" on the Underground Railroad. She led nineteen missions into the South in the years before the war to rescue 300 slaves. She also delivered lectures on the evils of slavery to northern audiences, and served as a Union spy during the Civil War. Many called her "Moses" for her dedication and bravery in leading blacks out of slavery.

Martin Van Buren Former secretary of state to Andrew Jackson, Van Buren was elected president on the Democratic ticket in 1836. Unfortunately for him, his years in office were plagued by a depression after the financial Panic of 1837. Believing that federal funds in smaller banks had made the economy worse, Van Buren pushed the Divorce Bill through congress to create an independent treasury. William Henry Harrison soundly defeated

him in the election of 1840. He also ran as the Free-Soil party candidate in
the election of 1848.

William Walker A proslavery American adventurer from the South, Walker led
an expedition to seize control of Nicaragua in 1855. Once in power, he
hoped to petition Franklin Pierce for annexation as a new slave state.
Unfortunately for him, several Latin American countries sent troops to
oust him before he could make the offer. The Nicaraguan adventurer was
just one example of Pierce's expansionist policies.

Suggested Reading

• Fehrenbacker, Don Edward. *Slavery, Law, and Politics: The Dred Scott Case in Historical Perspective.* New York: Oxford University Press, 1981.

This book is an in-depth and highly technical look at one of the Supreme Court's most embarrassing decisions. The average reader will be challenged by the heavy legal content, but Fehrenbacker's book provides an invaluable look at pre–Civil War America through the court case that put the issue of slavery front and center in American politics.

• Goodrich, Thomas. *War to the Knife: Bleeding Kansas, 1854–1861.* Mechanicsburg, Pennsylvania: Stackpole Books, 1998.

Goodrich examines the bloody battle between pro- and antislavery forces in Kansas that presaged the coming Civil War.

• Lincoln, Abraham and Stephen A. Douglas. *The Lincoln–Douglas Debates.* New York: Dover Publications, 2004.

This is a republication of the two speeches and seven debates between Lincoln and Douglas in 1858.

• Smith, Mark M. and Maurice Kirby, eds. *Debating Slavery: Economy and Society in the Antebellum American South.* New York: Cambridge University Press, 1998.

Smith provides insight into historians' claim that the South's economy would collapse without the institution of slavery.

• Waugh, John C. *On the Brink of Civil War: The Compromise of 1850 and How It Changed the Course of American History.* Wilmington, Delaware: Scholarly Resources, 2003.

Waugh lays bare the problems and consequences of the Compromise of 1850 and how it highlights the leading causes of the Civil War.

The Civil War: 1860–1865

- Lincoln and Secession
- The North
- The South
- The Early Years of the War
- The Turning Point
- The Final Year

9

The Civil War was the most catastrophic event in American history. More than 600,000 Americans died in the war, more than all those who died in every other American war combined. Though the war was bloody and horrendous, sometimes pitting father against son, it ultimately brought the North and South closer together.

Since the signing of the Constitution, the North and the South had developed into two distinct regions with two distinct economies and social structures. They had grown apart and were especially divided over the institution of slavery and individual states' rights versus the federal government. The war ended both debates, ensuring that slavery would perish and that federal power would dominate over states' rights, settling the sectional debate once and for all.

The Civil War proved to the world that democracy worked. Lincoln recognized the historical significance of the war even before he had won. In his Gettysburg Address, he argued that the outcome of the Civil War would determine the fate of representative government for the entire world. In his own words, ". . . we here highly resolve . . . that government of the people, by the people, for the people, shall not perish from the earth."

Lincoln and Secession

Very little held the United States together in 1860: the political parties had dissolved into sectional parties, and even churches had split over the slavery issue. People in the North simply couldn't understand the South's insistence on expanding the "slavocracy" westward, while southerners thought that northerners wanted to completely destroy their way of life. As a result, Americans on both sides of the Mason-Dixon Line wondered and worried about who would become the next president in 1860.

ELECTION OF 1860

Four candidates contended for the presidency in the election of 1860:

- **Abraham Lincoln** ran on the Republican ticket in favor of higher protective tariffs and more internal improvements, with promises to maintain the Union at all costs.

- **Stephen A. Douglas** ran for the northern Democratic Party, also on a pro-Union platform.

- **John C. Breckinridge** ran as a southern Democrat in strong support of slavery.

- **John Bell** ran with a breakaway group of compromising Republicans on the Constitutional Union Party ticket.

Because none of the slave states even put Lincoln's name on the ballot, the election eventually became two sectional elections, with Lincoln versus Douglas in the North and Breckinridge and Bell in the South. In the end, Lincoln won the presidency with approximately 39 percent of the popular vote, all eighteen free states, and a clear majority of 180 votes in the Electoral College.

SECESSION

Immediately after the election, South Carolina's legislature convened a special convention and voted unanimously to secede from the Union. South Carolina then issued **"A Declaration of the Causes of Secession,"** which reviewed the threats against slavery and asserted that a sectional party had elected a president hostile to slavery. By February 1861, six other slave states had followed suit, including Mississippi, Florida, Alabama, Georgia, Louisiana, and Texas.

The Crittenden Compromise

Hoping to prevent war, Senator John Crittenden from Kentucky proposed another compromise. He suggested adding an amendment to the Constitution to protect slavery in all territories South of 36° 30'. Popular sovereignty would determine whether the southwestern territories would enter the Union as free or slave states. Conversely, all territories north of 36° 30' would be free. Many southerners contemplated this **Crittenden Compromise**, but Lincoln rejected it out of the belief that the people had elected him to prevent the westward expansion of slavery.

Lincoln's First Inaugural Address

In his **First Inaugural Address**, Lincoln reaffirmed the North's friendship with the South, stressed national unity, and asked southerners to abandon secession. Moreover, he declared secession illegal and vowed to maintain the Union at all costs.

Fort Sumter

After declaring their independence, South Carolina authorities demanded the immediate withdrawal of all U.S. troops from **Fort Sumter**, a small island in Charleston Harbor. When Lincoln didn't comply, South Carolina militiamen shelled the fort on April 12, 1861, until the garrison's commander surrendered. Not a single soldier died during the fight, leading many southerners to conclude that northerners lacked the will to fight. The fall of Fort Sumter also convinced Arkansas, North Carolina, Tennessee, and Virginia to secede. The war had begun.

NORTHERN AND SOUTHERN ADVANTAGES

In retrospect, Union victory seems to have been inevitable. The Confederate struggle was doomed, lost in the romantic imagery of a lost cause, a small southern band fighting against a larger northern force. Large-scale industrialization, an enormous popu-

CHAPTER 9
1860–1865

lation, more resources, more weaponry, and a better transportation network gave the North a huge advantage. The Union also featured an efficient Navy and had the ability to build more ships. The Union quickly used its Navy to its advantage and blockaded southern ports.

At the time, however, these northern advantages seemed negligible because the South had superior military leaders, a captive labor force, hope for help from Europe, and the benefit of fighting a defensive war on familiar soil. As a result, both the North and the South naively believed they could defeat the other quickly and easily.

> The Civil War brutally tore families apart. One of Senator Crittenden's sons, for example, served as a general in the Union army, while another served as a general in the Confederacy. Even Abraham Lincoln himself had a brother-in-law fighting for the South.

The North

The Fall of Fort Sumter prompted Lincoln to prepare for war. He called for volunteers to enlist in the army and navy, ordered a naval blockade of southern ports, and moved troops to protect Washington, D.C. Congress later passed a number of sweeping measures to help industrialists and bolster the national economy.

THE BORDER STATES

Only ten of the fourteen slave states followed South Carolina and seceded from the Union. The other four—Maryland, Delaware, Kentucky, and Missouri—remained loyal to the United States. West Virginia eventually seceded from Virginia in 1863 and joined the Union as a free state. These five **border states** were crucial to the North because they geographically split the North from the South. Additionally, if the North were able to keep control of the border states, then they would discredit the Confederacy's claim that the Union would emancipate all slaves. Maryland and Delaware also had many factories that could have doubled the South's industrial capabilities, and Maryland's secession would have isolated Washington, D.C., from the rest of the North.

To ensure these states' loyalty, Lincoln sometimes had to resort to force to prevent them from joining the Confederacy. He suspended the **writ of habeas corpus** in Maryland, allowing the government to arrest suspected Confederate sympathizers and hold them without trial, and declared martial law in 1861 after pro-Confederacy protestors attacked U.S. soldiers marching to Washington, D.C.

BENDING THE CONSTITUTION

Lincoln also faced opposition from people in the North. On one side, **Peace Democrats** accused him of starting an unjust war, while **Radical Republicans** in his own party accused him of being too soft on the Confederacy. Many on both sides also criticized him for usurping unconstitutional powers to achieve his goals. Among other actions, Lincoln had suspended the writ of habeas corpus, ordered a naval blockade of all southern ports without Congress's permission, increased the size of the army without Congress's consent, and authorized illegal voting methods in the border states to ensure they wouldn't secede.

Chief Justice Roger Taney of the Supreme Court deemed these actions unconstitutional, but Lincoln ignored him, believing that desperate times called for drastic measures. Congress and most northerners generally approved of his decisions anyway.

THE 1862 CONGRESS

Congress, for its part, legislated a flurry of progressive new laws as soon as the South seceded from the Union. Without any states-rights advocates, northern Republicans easily passed the following acts:

- **The Morrill Tariff Act** to help northern manufacturers by doubling the prewar tariff on imported goods

- **The Legal Tender Act** to create a stable national currency

- **The National Banking Act** to strengthen banks and enforce the Legal Tender Act

These acts gave the federal government unprecedented power over the economy and provided stability to the robust industrial economy in the North, both of which ultimately helped the North defeat the South.

THE DRAFT AND DRAFT RIOTS

In 1863, Congress also passed a conscription law to draft young men into the Union Army. The law demanded that men either join the army or make a $300 contribution to the war effort. Although designed to promote support for the war among the rich and poor alike, this "$300 rule" effectively condemned the poorer classes to military service. Thousands of urban poor people staged protests against the law in dozens of northern cities. Protests in New York escalated into a full-scale riot in mid-1863, when racist whites from the poorest neighborhoods burned and looted parts of the city. Protestors also murdered nearly 100 people in the **New York City Draft Riot** before federal troops arrived.

THE NORTHERN ECONOMY

Throughout the war, northern factories continued to pump out weapons, clothing, and supplies for Union soldiers. Manufacturers increased production of agricultural equipment to help the farmers in the West produce more wheat and corn to feed the troops. The fields in the West benefited from good weather throughout the war, while the South suffered from extreme drought.

Oil production and coal mining became big industries in the North during these years as well. Alternatively, because the South had only a limited number of factories, Confederate troops often fought with antiquated weapons in tattered homespun uniforms and had little to eat.

Northern Women

In the North, women organized the United States Sanitary Commission to provide medical relief and other services to soldiers.

Other northern women worked to help starving and homeless freed slaves. Several thousand northern women also worked as nurses.

Almost 400 women disguised themselves as men and fought in the war as soldiers. Dozens also worked as spies. Women in the North and in the South played an increasing role in society and in the economy with men and sons away at war.

The South

Delegates from the first seven secessionist states (South Carolina, Mississippi, Alabama, Georgia, Florida, Texas, and Louisiana) met in Montgomery, Alabama, in February 1861 to form the government of the new **Confederate States of America** Using the U.S. Constitution as a template, they drafted a new constitution, chose Richmond, Virginia, to be the new capital, and selected Mississippi planter **Jefferson Davis** as the Confederacy's first president.

PRESIDENT DAVIS

Although Davis had more political experience than Lincoln (he'd served as secretary of war and as a U.S. senator), he proved to be a poor commander in chief. Unlike Lincoln, he didn't understand the importance of public opinion and as a result didn't connect well with voters. Moreover, his nervousness and refusal to delegate authority alienated many cabinet members, congressmen, and state governors. He often had difficulty controlling his own government.

FEDERATION VS. CONFEDERATION

Although the South used the U.S. Constitution as a model, the Confederate government differed radically from that of the United States, primarily because the drafters of the Confederate constitution wanted to protect the rights of the member states. To ensure that individual state governments would remain strong, southerners refused to give their federal government any real authority. In other words, the Richmond government more closely resembled a loose organization of strongly independent states rather than the tightly knit federation of the United States.

Keeping the Confederacy Together

Because the individual state governments in the South had more power than the central government, Davis had trouble controlling the states and coordinating the war. Lack of control proved to be the South's greatest weakness in the war for all of the following reasons:

- State governors refused to send their troops across state lines, even to assist in battle.

- State legislatures generally refused to support the Richmond government financially.

- A nation founded on secession couldn't logically withhold the right of member states to secede.

As a result, the central government in Richmond never had any money, lacked control over the national economy, couldn't maintain a strong national army, and couldn't even prevent states from seceding from the Confederacy during the final weeks of the war.

THE CONSCRIPTION ACT

The Richmond government passed the **Conscription Act of 1862** to force young men in all secessionist states into the national army. Like the draft in the North, the Confederate conscription law hurt poor people the most because it exempted wealthy planters and landowners.

Conscription Breeds Class Conflict

Although conscription eventually worked for the North despite the draft riots, it failed miserably in the South. Confederate regiments often suffered extremely heavy losses—and the poor southerners knew it. Poor soldiers resented the fact that they fought and bled in the war to support the rich whites who had started the war in the first place. They didn't see why they had to fight, and their own families had to starve, while the elites in Richmond ate well every night and slept safely and warmly in their beds. Not surprisingly, desertion unfolded as the southern military's greatest problem during the war.

COURTING GREAT BRITAIN

Davis hoped to end the war quickly by securing international recognition from Europe and possibly even a military alliance with Great Britain. He and most southerners realized that international recognition would legitimize the Confederacy and justify their cause. Moreover, an alliance with Britain would allow them to break the Union blockade that surrounded southern ports so that they could supply soldiers with weapons and food.

The Alabama and the Laird Rams

Because southern planters provided 75 percent of the cotton purchased by British textile manufacturers, Confederate policymakers thought Britain would certainly support them. For a time, Britain did harbor southern ships and even built Confederate warships, such as the **C.S.S. Alabama,** which eventually captured or sank more than sixty Union ships on the high seas. British shipbuilders also agreed to build two ironclad warships with **Laird rams** that the Confederate navy could use to pierce the hulls of enemy ships. Despite this assistance from Britain, Davis never managed to secure either official recognition or the alliance he so badly needed. This failure was due mainly to the following:

- British manufacturers had warehouses full of excess cotton shipments and didn't need southern cotton so urgently.
- British manufacturers had found other sources of cotton in India and Egypt.
- The poorer classes in England opposed slavery and thus opposed helping the South.
- Lincoln threatened to declare war on Britain if Britain helped the Confederacy.

As a result, the Laird rams were eventually scrapped, and Richmond lost all hope for help from Europe.

COLLAPSE OF THE SOUTHERN ECONOMY

Unable to break through the Union blockade around the southern ports, and thus unable to buy goods or sell cotton, the South witnessed its economy slide into a deep depression in 1862. Worse, inflation skyrocketed when the individual states and private banks printed more cheap paper money to counter the depression. The depression was so bad that many desperate women looted the Confederate capital in the **Richmond Bread Riots** of 1863 in search of food and out of anger at the inept central government.

> *The value of a single Confederate dollar hyperinflated so much that its value dropped by the minute. People standing in line to buy food quite often found themselves without enough money by the time they made it to the front of the line, because prices had changed. Tens of thousands of southerners consequently starved to death.*

Southern Women

As the southern economy collapsed, so too did southern society. The war's drastic effect on southern lives tore into the very fabric of society. Women, for example, took on traditionally masculine jobs while the men fought on the battlefield. Some women ran farms and plantations, some ran businesses, and some had to supervise slaves. Wealthier women, in particular, were jarred by the harsh reality of physical labor and rationing. Southern women had to be incredibly innovative and resourceful to feed, clothe, and shelter their families every day.

The Early Years of the War

Both the North and South hurried to create an army and navy after the fall of Fort Sumter, while thousands of men quickly enlisted out of fear they'd miss the fight. The initial enthusiasm and optimism, however, faded as soon as the "ninety-day war" turned into the bloodiest conflict in American history.

THE FIRST BATTLE OF BULL RUN

The first significant battle of the Civil War occurred at Manassas Junction, thirty miles southwest of Washington, D.C., in 1861. Civilians from both sides attended to watch the show, some even with picnic lunches. The battle proved far bloodier than anyone had expected when the Union soldiers fled and left several thousand dead and wounded behind. Dismayed, northerners buckled down for a long and bitter war, while southerners emerged with a false sense of strength.

THE BATTLE OF SHILOH

Just as the First Battle of Bull Run had shocked northerners, the Battle of Shiloh in April 1862 shattered southerners' hope for a quick and easy victory. Union General **Ulysses S. Grant** engaged Confederate forces at Shiloh, Tennessee, in a battle that killed tens of thousands of men. The eventual victory demonstrated Lincoln's unbending resolve to preserve the Union.

NAVAL BATTLES

The Confederate navy tried to break through the U.S. Navy's blockade with their new ironclad ship, the *Virginia*. Formerly an old Union warship named the *Merrimack*, southerners had salvaged the ship and refitted it with iron armor to make it impervious to cannonballs. The Union eventually developed its own ironclad, the *Monitor,* to destroy the *Virginia*. The two warships engaged in a battle in the Chesapeake Bay in 1862, and though neither ship achieved a clear victory, the so-called **Battle of the Ironclads** marked the beginning of a new era in naval warfare.

The Union Navy continued to tighten its grip on the South and eventually freed the lower Mississippi by seizing New Orleans from the Confederates. The Navy then began working its way up the Mississippi River to tear the Confederacy in two.

THE BATTLE OF ANTIETAM

In September 1862, Union and Confederate forces engaged each other in the **Battle of Antietam. Robert E. Lee**, the

CHAPTER 9
1860–1865

Confederate General, trying to move the war into the North, had crossed the Potomac with 40,000 men. Union General **George McClellan** moved his troops to meet Lee in western Maryland. Tens of thousands of soldiers died during the single bloodiest day of the entire war. An aide to Union General George McClellan had actually found Lee's battle plan prior to the engagement, but McClellan chose not to make full use of the information. Despite this missed opportunity, Lee was eventually forced to move his tattered army back across the Potomac to Virginia.

Lincoln Fires McClellan

As commander of the Army of the Potomac in Washington, D.C., George McClellan was the highest-ranking general in the Union army even though he had not yet reached forty. Despite his popularity with the troops, the civilian leaders in Washington disliked him because he seemed to avoid fighting battles. Lincoln needed military victories and wanted to end the war as quickly as possible—he knew voters wouldn't support a long and drawn-out war.

To make matters worse, as the war entered its second year, McClellan grew increasingly critical of Lincoln and the Republicans. He made personal jabs against the president in public and privately speculated that only he, personally, could end the war and save the Union. Lincoln eventually fired the disobedient and overly cautious McClellan and filled his post with several other incompetent generals before finally naming Ulysses S. Grant commander of all Union forces.

Antietam's Significance

Lee's failure at Antietam proved incredibly costly for the South because it convinced Britain and France not to support the Confederacy in the Civil War. Without international recognition or military assistance, Davis had little hope of breaking the Union blockade or defeating the Union army. The North's victory at Antietam also gave Lincoln the opportunity to issue the Emancipation Proclamation.

EMANCIPATION

Lincoln decided in 1862 to emancipate the slaves held in areas under Confederate control for three reasons:

- Slave labor helped sustain the Confederacy economically.

- Turning the war into a moral cause would boost support for the war in the North.

- Emancipation would ensure that Britain and France would not enter the war.

Although Lincoln did view slavery as a moral evil, he issued the Emancipation Proclamation not out of love for blacks, but because he thought it would help the Union defeat the Confederacy. In fact, he once remarked, "If I could save the Union without freeing any slave, I would do it; and if I could save it by freeing all the slaves, I would do it; and if I could do it by freeing some and leaving others alone, I would also do that. What I do about Slavery and the colored race, I do because I believe it helps to save this Union."

Emancipation Proclamation

Although first issued in September 1862, the **Emancipation Proclamation** actually took effect on January 1, 1863. The proclamation:

- Freed all slaves behind Confederate lines

- Did not free any slaves in the border states

- Allowed free blacks to join the U.S. army and navy

Slavery had been at the root of every sectional conflict since delegates had made the Three-Fifths Compromise at the Constitutional Convention in 1787. Lincoln needed to cure the disease that had caused the war, not just treat the symptoms. Even though the proclamation didn't emancipate slaves in the border states—Lincoln didn't want any of them to secede in anger—it did mark the beginning of the end for the "peculiar institution" for every state in the Union. Democrats, meanwhile, criticized Lincoln for wedding the goals of emancipation and reunification.

CHAPTER 9

1860–1865

About 180,000 African Americans served in the United States Colored Troops division, or roughly 10 percent of the army. Around 30,000 more blacks served in the U.S. Navy, making one out of every four sailors African American.

The Turning Point

The year 1863 marked a turning point in the war and the beginning of the end for the Confederacy. Not coincidentally, it was also the year that Lincoln's search for a capable general ended with the selection of Ulysses S. Grant.

SIEGE OF VICKSBURG

Ulysses S. Grant was a General in the Union Army at the beginning of 1863, in charge of troops trying to gain control of the Mississippi River. Grant turned the tide of the war in the West after laying siege to the port city of Vicksburg, Mississippi, on the Mississippi River. Having been unable to conquer Confederate forces protecting the city, Grant chose instead to merely surround the city and wait until starvation forced the Confederates to surrender, which they did on July 4, 1863, Independence Day.

Many historians agree that the surrender of Vicksburg was the most important Union victory of the war. The surrender gave the Union control of the Mississippi River and split the Confederacy in half. Subsequently, Lincoln promoted the victorious Grant to commander of all Union forces.

BATTLE OF GETTYSBURG

As fate would have it, the Union achieved not one, but two major victories on Independence Day in 1863. While Grant was accepting Vicksburg's surrender in Mississippi, Union forces were repelling Robert E. Lee's invasion into Pennsylvania at the **Battle of Gettysburg**. After three days of some of the bloodiest fighting in the war, Lee retreated back to Confederate territory, leaving a

Unlike his southern counterpart Robert E. Lee, Ulysses S. Grant lacked a distinguished pedigree and had been only an average student at West Point. In fact, he'd even been court-martialed and discharged from the army for being drunk while on duty. He later volunteered in a local militia when the Civil War broke out, where he eventually caught Lincoln's eye. Grant achieved so many victories on the battlefield that when critics accused him of alcoholism, President Lincoln merely retorted, "Find out what he is drinking and send a case of it to my other generals."

third of his entire army among the 50,000 soldiers that lay dead or wounded on the battlefield.

*Lincoln commemorated the Union victory at Gettysburg with a short speech simply known as the **Gettysburg Address**. In the speech, Lincoln argued that the outcome of the Civil War would be of the utmost importance for the entire world because it would prove whether democracy could work.*

Death Knell for the South

Lee's defeat at Gettysburg crushed the South: twice the South had invaded the North, and twice it had failed (at Antietam and Gettysburg). The loss of the Mississippi at the Battle of Vicksburg proved even more damaging in the long run because it deprived southerners of their primary mode of transportation in the West.

The Union victories also boosted morale and support for the war in the North and increased Lincoln's popularity. In addition, the Union blockade's chokehold on the South had finally begun to take its toll on the southern economy. By 1863, the Confederacy couldn't trade cotton for war supplies or food. Still, Davis continued to wage war for two more years hoping that chance, providence, or Great Britain would help him.

Davis continued to fight in the hope that a long and protracted war would eventually turn northern public opinion against Lincoln and the war itself. He particularly hoped Lincoln would lose his bid for reelection in 1864 to the Peace Democrats, who would end the war and leave the South alone.

CHAPTER 9
1860–1865

The Final Year

As the fighting dragged on into its fourth year, Lincoln felt increasing pressure to end the war. He knew that even the fieriest abolitionists couldn't tolerate much more bloodshed. As a result, Lincoln put more pressure on his generals to bear down on the Confederacy with as much military might as possible and end the war quickly.

SHERMAN'S MARCH TO THE SEA

Abraham Lincoln and Ulysses S. Grant knew the South had to be defeated soon if they ever hoped to restore the Union. In 1864, Grant ordered his close friend and fellow general **William Tecumseh Sherman** to take a small force through the heart of the Deep South and destroy everything in his path. Grant hoped that this destruction would bring the South to its knees. Sherman embarked on his famous **March to the Sea** that summer, burning the city of Atlanta and then marching toward Savannah, Georgia. Along the way, he destroyed railroads, burned homes, razed crops, and looted, plundered, and pillaged the entire countryside. Sherman eventually seized Savannah and then marched northward to South Carolina.

> Sherman fought a **total war** against the South, waging war directly on civilians by plundering, marauding, and destroying the landscape. He hoped that extreme hardship would eventually break the southerners' will to continue fighting and force them to surrender.

GROWING OPPOSITION IN THE NORTH

A growing number of **Peace Democrats** had meanwhile begun to call for an immediate end to the war. More commonly known as **Copperheads**, after the poisonous snake, these Democrats believed that Lincoln and his generals had adequately demonstrated the futility of the war. Many Copperheads in the prosouthern **"Butternut region"** in Ohio, Indiana, and Illinois felt outraged that Lincoln had turned the conflict into a war over slavery. **Radical Republicans** in his own party criticized Lincoln because they thought the Emancipation Proclamation should have freed all slaves South *and* North.

THE ELECTION OF 1864

As a result, bitterness and uncertainty clouded the crucial election of 1864. Democrats who supported the war joined Republicans in giving Lincoln a lukewarm nomination for a second term, despite opposition from the radicals. Lincoln chose War Democrat Andrew Johnson from the conquered state of Tennessee as his running mate in the hope that Johnson would win more votes from Democrats in the North.

Together, Lincoln and Johnson campaigned on a simple platform for continuation of the war until the South surrendered unconditionally. Peace Democrats, on the other hand, nominated former general George McClellan on an equally simple platform calling for immediate peace. In the end, Lincoln won with 55 percent of the popular vote.

A Mandate for Unconditional Surrender

The election of 1864 was in many ways the most crucial event during the entire conflict. The election determined the outcome of the war; if McClellan and the Peace Democrats had won, the war would have ended immediately. The election ruined the Confederacy's last hope for survival. Lincoln's reelection provided a clear mandate from northern voters for unconditional surrender. Surprisingly, many of the soldiers themselves—Democrat as well as Republican—had voted for Lincoln because they wanted to finish what they had begun.

THE SOUTH COLLAPSES

The South, meanwhile, was on the brink of collapse. The naval blockade, refusals for assistance from Britain, Sherman's March, internal class conflicts, and the complete meltdown of southern society and the economy had taken their toll. Thousands of men deserted the army daily as thousands more southern women and children starved at home. Jefferson Davis tried desperately to hold his government together, but none of the states would cooperate. In the final month of the war, the South grew so desperate that they even began offering slaves their freedom if they would enlist in the Confederate army.

The Hampton Roads Conference

In one final attempt to save the Confederacy, Davis requested a ceasefire to discuss peace. Lincoln agreed and sent a delegation to the **Hampton Roads Conference** in February 1865. Negotiations quickly ended, however, because Lincoln refused to settle for anything less than unconditional surrender, which Davis refused to give.

APPOMATTOX

In April 1865, Grant's forces broke through Robert E. Lee's defenses and burned the Confederate capital at Richmond. With his men half starved and heavily outgunned, Lee chose to surrender rather than send his remaining troops to their death. Grant accepted Lee's unconditional surrender at Appomattox Courthouse on April 9, 1865 and provided the southerners with food for their march home. Union troops captured Jefferson Davis and other ranking Confederates as they tried to flee Virginia. The Civil War had ended.

THE ASSASSINATION OF LINCOLN

Lincoln lived just long enough to see the war's end. **John Wilkes Booth**, a southern sympathizer, assassinated the president on April 14, 1865, as he sat with his wife in a box at Ford's Theater in Washington, D.C., mere days after Grant accepted Lee's surrender at Appomattox. Booth shot Lincoln and then jumped down to the stage below, shouting, *"Sic semper tyrannis,"* a Latin phrase meaning "thus always to tyrants."

The political debate about slavery began at the
Constitutional Convention in 1787 and continued until
1860 and the start of the Civil War. Evaluate the growing
political discord over slavery and the rise of sectionalism
from 1787 until 1860.

The debate about slavery changed radically between the early
colonial period and the start of the Civil War. There was little
controversy when the first African slaves were brought to Virginia
in 1619. It was only at the Constitutional Convention of 1787 that
slavery became the subject of any serious political discussion.
From that time, however, it was a matter of increasing concern.
Over the coming decades, the debate underwent three stages. It
began as an argument over theoretical principles, then grew more
and more tied to economics, and finally became the focus of a
heated dispute over morality versus states' rights to choose their
own policies.

The political debate over slavery started out mainly as one of
principle. More than a third of the delegates in attendance at the
Constitutional Convention of 1787 were slaveholders themselves,
but they all shared the view that the country needed a stronger
national government. This was their primary concern, and a spirit
of compromise characterized the deliberations. The delegates
carefully deferred decisions that would have broad consequences
for slavery and focused their debate upon the issue of
congressional representation, and on whether slaves should be
counted in a state's population. Even this matter was settled with
a compromise, and the delegates agreed that three-fifths of a
state's slaves would be counted toward its population. This
conciliatory attitude characterized the early stages of the debate
over slavery up until the Missouri Compromise of 1820. In this
arrangement, the admission of Missouri as a slave state was offset
by the admission of Maine as a free state. Furthermore, both sides
agreed that slavery would be prohibited in the remainder of the
Louisiana Territory north of the 36° 30' parallel west of Missouri.

Student Essay

Both sides made difficult concessions, but were willing to work with each other.

However, the debate slowly took on a new urgency as the nation began to follow separate paths of economic development. The invention of the cotton gin in 1793 revolutionized the agrarian South, and its economy became ever more dependent upon slavery as a source of manual labor. Meanwhile, the North pursued the path of industrialization and urbanization. As the two regions grew further apart economically, the North was harboring a belief that the South was clinging to tradition and resisting the movement toward progress. The regional differences came head to head in 1828 with the Tariff of Abominations. On behalf of the South, Vice-President John Calhoun argued that the high protective tariff favored industry in the North at the expense of the South. Likewise, he believed that the tariff was unconstitutional because it did not advance the good of the whole country. Calhoun implied that if the government was capable of promoting the interests of one region over another, southern slavery might be the next victim. The anxiety about slavery in the South was compounded by the rise of the abolition movement in the North. While the spirit of compromise still existed, the first rumblings about secession and the possibility of civil war could also be heard.

The possibility for compromise finally died when morality emerged as the central element of the debate over slavery. The abolition movement led by William Lloyd Garrison adamantly maintained that slavery was immoral, and that all slaves should be liberated. The growing political voice of the abolition movement, which culminated in the formation of the Free Soil Party, caused great concern in the South. Fully understanding the cultural and economic implications of abolition, many southerners viewed the North with increasing suspicion. Sectional differences peaked as the Manifest Destiny movement took hold of the country. New states such as Oregon and Texas were admitted to the Union, followed by the lands won in the Mexican–American War. This aroused a fierce debate about slavery in these new territories that would soon become states, as each side hoped to secure a majority representation in Congress. Although the Compromise of 1850 provided some relief by restoring the balance between free states and slave states, it also introduced the idea of popular sovereignty, allowing residents of the territory to decide if they would have slaves or be a free state. Ultimately, the tenuous harmony collapsed with the Kansas–Nebraska Act, which effectively nullified the Missouri Compromise. With both sides fighting for their very way of existence, political compromise was no longer an option. The stage was set for civil war.

Prior to the Missouri Compromise, the political debate about slavery transcended regional differences. Delegates at the Constitutional Convention deliberately chose not to make specific provisions regulating slavery and instead set a precedent for the kind of political compromise illustrated by the Missouri Compromise. However, the Kansas-Nebraska Act undermined the boundary that was agreed to in the Missouri Compromise, creating an insurmountable obstacle. In the three decades separating those two acts, the North and South had diverged economically, culturally, and politically to the point where civil war was all but inevitable.

Test Questions and Answers

1. Why did Lincoln win the election of 1860? How did southerners react?

- Lincoln won the election because no candidate could command a national following.

- There were virtually two different races for the presidency: Breckinridge versus Bell in the South, and Douglas versus Lincoln in the North.

- South Carolina seceded almost immediately after Lincoln's victory in 1860.

- Several other southern states quickly followed.

2. What was the significance of the Emancipation Proclamation? What effect did it have on the North and on the South?

- The proclamation emancipated only those blacks still enslaved by the Confederacy, *not* those enslaved in the pro-Union border states.

- It irrevocably linked the abolition of slavery to the Union cause.

- It angered some northerners, like Peace Democrats and Radical Republicans.

- It demoralized the South, especially in the wake of Lee's retreat at Antietam.

3. Why were the border states so important to Lincoln?

- They physically separated the Union and the Confederacy.

- Maryland prevented Washington, D.C., from falling under Confederate control.

- Maryland's and Delaware's decision to remain in the Union cut the South's industrial capabilities in half.

- Maryland's and Delaware's decision to remain in the Union damaged the Confederacy's claim that Lincoln and the Union wanted to eliminate slavery.

4. *Compare and contrast Abraham Lincoln and Jefferson Davis as wartime presidents.*

- Lincoln usually understood the importance of public opinion, whereas Davis did not.

- Lincoln exerted much more influence and control over his government than Davis did in Richmond.

- Davis often appeared nervous and lost his temper easily, whereas Lincoln usually remained calm, collected, and in control.

Timeline

1860	Abraham Lincoln is elected president.
	South Carolina secedes from the Union.
1861	Alabama, Arkansas, Florida, Georgia, Louisiana, Mississippi, North Carolina, Tennessee, Texas, and Virginia secede.
	North Carolina, Tennessee, Texas, and Virginia secede.
	South Carolina attacks Ft. Sumter.
	The first significant battle of the Civil War occurs at the Battle of Bull Run.
1862	Congress passes the Legal Tender Act.
	Confederacy passes the Conscription Act.
	Congress passes the Confiscation Act.
	The Union defeats the Confederacy at the Battle of Antietam.
1863	Lincoln's *Emancipation Proclamation* takes effect.
	Congress passes the National Bank Act.
	Drafts are initiated in the North.
	Southern women loot the Confederate capital in the Richmond Bread Riots in Richmond, Virginia.
	Nearly 100 people are murdered in the Draft Riots in New York City.
	The Battle of Gettysburg crushes the South.
	The Siege of Vicksburg gives the Union control of the Mississippi River.
1864	Grant takes command of Union troops.
	Lincoln is reelected.
	Sherman begins his March to the Sea.
1865	Davis proposes Hampton Roads peace conference.
	Robert E. Lee surrenders to Grant at Appomattox Courthouse.
	Abraham Lincoln is assassinated.

Major Figures

John Bell The Constitutional Union Party candidate for president, Bell ran against Abraham Lincoln, Stephen Douglas, and John C. Breckinridge in the election of 1860. Bell campaigned for compromise, Union, and slavery. He received wide support in the border states region, but carried only Kentucky, Virginia, and Tennessee.

John C. Breckinridge When the Democratic Party split after the 1860 nominating convention failed to select a presidential candidate, southern Democrats met separately in Charleston and nominated Breckinridge. Although Breckinridge claimed to desire unity and compromise, what he really wanted was a northern concession for the westward expansion of slavery. In the following election of 1860, he carried nine states—all of them in the South.

Jefferson Davis A former Senator from Mississippi, Davis was selected to be the first president of the Confederacy in 1861. Overworked and underappreciated by his fellow Confederates, Davis struggled throughout the Civil War to unify the southern states under the central government.

Stephen Douglas A Democratic senator from Illinois, Douglas pushed the Kansas–Nebraska Act through Congress in 1854 to entice railroad developers to build a transcontinental railroad line in the North. The act opened Kansas and Nebraska territories to slavery and thus effectively repealed the Missouri Compromise of 1820. Douglas rejected the proslavery Lecompton Constitution in the Senate in 1857 after Border Ruffians had rigged the elections to draft a state constitution. A champion of popular sovereignty, he announced his Freeport Doctrine in response to the Dred Scott decision in the Lincoln–Douglas debates against Abraham Lincoln in 1858. Although he was the most popular Democrat, southern party members refused to nominate him for the presidency in 1860 because he had rejected the Lecompton Constitution to make Kansas a slave state. As a result, the party split: northern Democrats nominated Douglas, while southern Democrats nominated John C. Breckinridge. In the election of 1860, Douglas toured the country in an effort to save the Union.

Ulysses S. Grant Nicknamed "Unconditional Surrender" Grant after his successes as the Union's top general in the Civil War, Grant became a Republican and entered politics during the Reconstruction years. He briefly served as secretary of war after Andrew Johnson had fired Edwin M. Stanton, but resigned when Stanton was reinstated. In 1868, he defeated Horatio Seymour to become the eighteenth president of the United States. Although he was himself honest, Grant's cabinet was filled with corruption, and his presidency was marred by scandals such as the Fisk-Gould gold scheme, Crédit Mobilier, and the Whiskey Ring. He retired after his second term.

Robert E. Lee Arguably the most brilliant general in the U.S. Army in 1860, Lee turned down Abraham Lincoln's offer to command the Union forces during the Civil War in favor of commanding the Army of northern Virginia for the Confederacy. Although he loved the United States, he felt he had to stand by his native state of Virginia. His defeat at the Battle of Gettysburg was the turning point in the war in favor of the North. He made the Confederacy's unconditional surrender at Appomattox Courthouse to Ulysses S. Grant in April 1865 to end the Civil War.

Abraham Lincoln A former lawyer from Illinois, Lincoln became the sixteenth president of the United States in the election of 1860. Because he was a Republican and associated with the abolitionist cause, his election prompted South Carolina to become the first state to secede from the Union. Lincoln believed that the states had legally never truly left the Union, but fought the war until the South surrendered unconditionally. He proposed the Ten-Percent Plan for Reconstruction in 1863, but was assassinated by John Wilkes Booth before he could carry out his plans.

George McClellan A young, first-rate U.S. Army general, McClellan commanded roughly 100,000 Union troops in Washington D.C. Unfortunately for Abraham Lincoln, McClellan proved to be overly cautious and was always reluctant to engage Confederate forces at a time when the president badly needed military victories to satisfy northern public opinion. He did manage to defeat Robert E. Lee at the Battle of Antietam in 1862, which gave Lincoln the opportunity to issue the Emancipation Proclamation. Lincoln eventually fired McClellan after the general began to publicly criticize the president's ability to command. McClellan ran for president as a Peace Democrat on a platform for peace against Lincoln, but was defeated.

William Tecumseh Sherman A close friend of Ulysses S. Grant, Sherman served as a general in the Union Army during the Civil War. Like Grant, he understood that the war would only truly be won when southerners' will to fight had been broken. He and his expedition force waged a total war on the South during his March to the Sea from Atlanta to Savannah, burning cities and crops, destroying railroad ties, and liberating slaves. His harsh tactic helped break the South and end the war.

Suggested Reading

- Burns, Ken. *The Civil War*. DVD. Directed by Burns. Arlington, Virginia: WETA-TV, 2002.

This award-winning documentary on the Civil War includes narration by several well-known historians and is also a moving portrait of the lives of regular soldiers on both sides of the conflict.

- Faust, Drew Gilpin. *Mothers of Invention: Women of the Slaveholding South in the American Civil War*. New York: Vintage Books, 1996.

During the Civil War, women in the South were thrust into areas previously reserved for men only, including the farm, the economy, and other social areas. Faust examines the lives these women led in the South in the pre–Civil War era and throughout the war, especially as the Union Army pushed farther and farther south.

- Gienapp, William E. *Abraham Lincoln and Civil War America: A Biography*. New York: Oxford University Press, 2002.

More of an examination of Lincoln as president during the Civil War than a biography, Gienapp examines the short life and incredible impact of one of the nation's youngest presidents in one of the United States' most horrific eras.

- McPherson, James. *Battle Cry of Freedom: The Civil War Era*. New York: Oxford University Press, 1988.

This Pulitzer Prize–winning book about the Civil War has long been the standard to which all books about the Civil war are held. McPherson's work covers the major battles in great detail, but also touches upon the social and political aspects that led to the war.

- ———. *The Negro's Civil War: How American Blacks Felt and Acted During the War for the Union*. New York: Vintage Books, 2003.

McPherson examines the role that blacks played in the Civil War, denouncing the myth that blacks were inactive bystanders in the fight for their freedom.

INDEX

Anti-Abolitionism, in the North, 179
Anti-Federalists, 95
Anti-Masonic Party, 147–148
  primary objective of, 148
Anti-prostitution societies, 180
Appomattox Courthouse, 232, 239
Arbella (ship), 22
Arthur, T. S., 180, 189
Articles of Confederation, 4, 87–92, 94, 109
  Continental dollars and depression, 89–90
  governing western lands, 89
  Shays's Rebellion, 89–90
  weak national government, 88–89
Assumption, 97
Asylum reform, 181
Aztecs, 11, 14, 30

B

Bacon, Nathaniel, 19, 31
Bacon's Rebellion, 18–19, 26–27, 30
Bank of the United States, 98, 109, 142, 163
Bank War and Tariff crisis, 5
Baptists, 176
  growth of, in the colonies, 47
Battle of Antietam, 225–226, 239
  significance of, 226
Battle of Buena Vista, 156
Battle of Bull Run, 239
Battle of Fallen Timbers, 100, 109
Battle of Gettysburg, 228–229, 239
Battle of Lexington and Concord, 71, 73, 80, 83
Battle of New Orleans, 123, 124
Battle of Saratoga, 83
Battle of Tippecanoe, 121, 134
Battle of Yorktown, 77

Bell, John, 216, 240
Bering Strait, 10
Beringia, 10
Berkeley, William, 18–19
Bill of Rights, 96, 109
"Biological exchange," Spanish exploration, 14
Birney, James G., 153
Black Hawk War (1832), 149, 163
Blacks, *See* African Americans:
Bleeding Kansas crisis, 4, 199–200, 204–205, 209
Bonaparte, Napoleon, 118, 122
Book of Mormon, 177
Booth, John Wilkes, 232
Border Ruffians, 199, 201
Border states, 218–219
Boston Massacre, 68, 70, 83
Boston Port Act, 69
Boston Tea Party, 69, 70, 79, 83
Boycott, 67, 70
Brant, Joseph, 75, 84
Breckinridge, John C., 216, 240
Brook Farm commune, 178, 188
Brooks, Preston, 199
Brown, John, 199, 209–210
Buchanan, James, 200–201, 209, 210
  and the Kansas-Nebraska crisis, 198–201
Buena Vista, battle of, 156
Bull Run, battle of, 239
Bunker Hill, 80
  battle of, 83
Buren, Martin Van, 150, 151, 158, 163, 167, 173, 188, 194, 212–213
  and the Divorce Bill, 151
Burned-Over District, 176
Burr, Aaron, 116
"Butternut region," 230–231

C

Calhoun, John C., 121, 124, 136, 163, 165, 210, 235
  South Carolina exposition, 145
California:
  admission to the Union, 195
  Gold Rush, 195
  Polk's ambition to add to the Union, 154
Cartier, Jacques, 15, 31
Cass, Lewis, 194, 210
Central and South American Natives, 10–12
Champlain, Samuel de, 15, 31
Checks and balances, 6–7, 94, 106
Cherokee Nation v. Georgia, 149
Cherokees, 11, 75, 121
  and the Indian Removal Act, 149
Chesapeake Affair, 120
Chesapeake (warship), 120
Chickasaws, 11, 121, 149
Choctaws, 11, 75, 121, 149
Church of Latter Day Saints, 177
Citizen Genêt affair, 101, 109
"City Upon a Hill" sermon (Winthrop), 6, 22, 30
Civil rights, 7
Civil War, 2, 5, 105, 181, 200, 215–242
  Abraham Lincoln, and secession, 216–18
  Battle of Antietam, 225–226
    significance of, 226
  Battle of Bull Run, 225
  Battle of Gettysburg, 228–229
  Battle of Shiloh, 225
  Battle of the Ironclads, 225
  Congress of 1862, 219
  early years of, 224–228
  election of 1864, 230
  Emancipation Proclamation, 226–227, 231, 240
  growing opposition to the war in the North, 230–231
  Lincoln fires McClellan, 226

  naval battles, 225
  North, 218–221
    border states, 218–219
    draft and draft riots, 220
    economy, 220–221
    women, 220–221
  Northern and Southern advantages, 218
  prelude to, 193–213
  siege of Vicksburg, 228
  South, 221–224
    collapse of, 232
    death knell for, 229
    economy, collapse of, 224
    federation vs. confederation, 221–222
    keeping the Confederacy together, 222–223
    President Jefferson Davis, 221
    women, 224, 239
  student essay, 204–206, 234–236
  unconditional surrender, mandate for, 231
Clark, William, 119
Class conflict, and conscription, 222–223
Clay, Henry, 4, 121, 124, 136, 142–143, 150, 151, 153, 165, 171, 195, 210–211
  American System, 124–125
  and the Compromise Tariff (1833), 146
  and the election of 1832, 147–148
  Missouri Compromise, 128–129
  and the Second Bank of the United States (SBUS), 147
Clinton, William Jefferson "Bill," 22
Coercive Acts, 69–70, 79, 83
Cohens v. Virginia, 127
Colonial life (1700–1763), 35–59
  British rule, 48–51
  British trade with the colonies, 48–50
  cities, 40
  class stratification, 40
  colonial cities, 40
  colonial governments, 50–51
    voting and representation, 51
  culture of the colonies, 48

Declaration of Independence, 1, 44–45, 72–73, 115

Declaration of Sentiments, Seneca Falls (N.Y.) Convention, 182

"Declaration of the Causes of Secession, A," 216

Declaration of the Rights and Grievances of the Colonies, 67

Declaratory Act, 67, 83

Deere, John, 171, 188

Delaware, 25
colonies of, 50

Democratic-Republicans, 4, 99, 101, 104, 105, 106, 115, 143

Depression:
and Continental dollars, 89–90
and Martin Van Buren, 151

Dickinson, Emily, 6

Discovery of the New World, 13

Divorce Bill, 151, 212

Dix, Dorothea, 181, 188, 190

Douglas, Stephen A., 195, 198, 201, 206, 209, 211, 216, 240
and the Kansas-Nebraska crisis, 196–198
Lincoln-Douglas Debates, 202–203

Douglass, Frederick, 178

Drafts, initiation of, 239

Dred Scott case, 2

Dred Scott decision, 209
backlash to, 202

Dred Scott v. Sanford, 202

Dunkers, 25

Dutch, and slavery, 41

Dutch Mennonites, 24

Dutch Reformed, 24, 25

Dwight, Timothy, 176

E

Early European exploration, 12–15

Early prohibition, 180

East India Company, 68–69

Economic vision, of Alexander Hamilton, 98

Economy, 3
and Alexander Hamilton, 97–98

Economy of the South, collapse of, 224

Education reform, 178, 181

Edwards, Jonathan, 46–47, 59, 60

"Elastic clause," 98

Elections:
of 1796, 102–103
of 1800, 116–117
of 1808, 120–121
of 1832, 147–148
of 1836, 150
of 1840, 151
of 1844, 152
of 1848, 194
of 1856, 200
of 1860, 216
of 1864, 231

Electoral College, 93, 96, 116, 143, 216

Elizabeth I, queen of England, 16

Emancipation Proclamation, 226–227, 231, 239

Embargo Act (1807), 119–120, 134

Emerson, Ralph Waldo, 183, 190

Encomienda system, 14–15

England (Great Britain):
British rule over the colonies, 48–51
British trade with the colonies, 48–50
Davis's courting of, 223
English dominance in North America, 16–25
Jamestown settlement, 17–19
Massachusetts Bay Company, 21
middle colonies, 23–25
and slavery, 41
war debt, 65–66

English Quakers, 25

Enlightenment, 44–45, 182

George III, king of England, 50, 65, 67, 69, 70–72, 78, 80, 84
  "abuses and usurpations" against the American colonies, 73
  intolerance to American resistance, 71
Georgia, 36
German and Irish immigration, 174–175
German Baptists, 24
German Hessian mercenaries, 76
Gettysburg, battle of, 228–229, 239
Gettysburg Address, 6, 215, 228–229
Gibbons v. Ogden, 127, 135
Gilbert, Sir Humphrey, 16–17
Gold Rush, 3, 195
Government, struggle to define the role of, 4–5
Grant, Ulysses S., 156, 225, 240–241
  Appomattox, 232–233
  criticisms of, 229
  education of, 228
  and Sherman's March to the Sea, 230
  and the siege of Vicksburg, 228
Great Awakening, 46–47, 59
  impact of, 47
Great Compromise, 92
Greene, Nathaniel, 74
Grenville, George, 65–66, 84
Gutenberg, Johann, 12, 30

H

Halfway Covenant, 23, 26, 30
Hamilton, Alexander, 3, 4, 92, 95, 96–97, 102, 106, 109, 110
  economic vision, 98
  and the economy, 97–98
  excise tax, 98
  national bank, 98
Hamiltonian Federalists, 99

Hampton Roads Conference, 232, 239
Hancock, John, 71
Harper's Ferry, 203, 209
Harrison, William Henry, 121, 136, 150, 151, 163, 164, 165–166, 212–213
Hartford Convention, 123, 134
Hawthorne, Nathaniel, 183, 189
Henry, Patrick, 91, 95, 106
Hispaniola, Columbus's discovery of, 13
Hopi tribe, 11
House of Representatives, 93
  gag resolution, passage of, 179
Hudson River School, 183
Hugh Lawson White, 150
Hutchinson, Thomas, 66, 69

I

Impressment, 120
Incas, 11
Indentured servants, 18, 36
Independence, 63–77
Indian Intercourse Act (1790), 99–100, 109, 121
Indian Removal Act (1830), 2, 148–149, 163, *See also* Native Americans
  and Andrew Jackson, 148–149
  Native American resistance to, 149
  "Trail of Tears," 149
Industrial Revolution, 170
Insane-asylum reform, 181
Interchangeable parts, 170–171
Internal improvements, 125
Intolerable Acts (1773), 69–70
Iroquois, 11, 75
Isabella, queen of Spain, 13
Isthmus of Panama, civilizations that developed near, 10–11

INDEX

discovery of, 13
first map of, 14
Jamestown settlement, 17
New York, 24
New York City Draft Riots, 220,
239
Newton, Isaac, 44
Ninth Amendment, 96
Non-Intercourse Act (1809),
122, 134
Nonwhites, exclusion from
American society, 2–3
North, Civil War, 218–221
border states, 218–219
draft and draft riots, 220
economy, 220–221
women, 220–221
North America, civilizations that
emerged in, 11
North Carolina, 36
Northern colonies, 37–38
crops grown in, 38
geography of the North, 38
life in, 39
new roles for women, 40
religion in, 39
Salem Witch trials, 39–40
work in, 38–39
North, Frederick Lord, 68
Northern denominations, 177
Northern society, 173–174
German and Irish immigration,
174–175
strikes and reforms, 173
wage labor system, 173
Northwest Confederacy, 121
Northwest Ordinance (1787),
89, 109
Nullification crisis, 5, 144–146
Nullification Proclamation, 146,
163
and Andrew Jackson, 146

O

Oberlin College, admission of
women to, 181, 188
Olive Branch Petition, 71, 78, 80
Oneida Community, 178, 189
Opening of the West, 3
Oregon Trail, 154, 169
Oregon Treaty (1846), 154
Ostend Manifesto, 197, 209

P

Paine, Thomas, 74, 83, 84, 176
Panic of 1819, 127, 134, 147
Panic of 1837, 150–151, 163, 212
Panic of 1857, 209
Parliament, 51
and the colonists, 66
and the Declaratory Act, 66
Peace Democrats, 219, 229, 230
Peace of Paris, 54, 83
Penn, William, 25, 50
Pennsylvania, 25
colonies of, 50
Pequot tribe, 11
Pierce, Franklin, 197, 209, 211–
213
Pilgrims, 19–21
assistance from Native Americans,
20
first Thanksgiving holiday, 20
London Virginia Company, 21
Massachusetts Bay Company,
21–23
Mayflower Compact, 21
Mayflower voyage, 20
New World freedom, 19–20
Plymouth Virginia Company, 21
and the Wampanoag Indians, 20
Pinckney, Charles C., 116, 120
Pinckney's Treaty, 101, 109
Pitt, William, 54–55
Pizarro, Francisco, 14, 30, 31
Plantation owners, and politics,
205–206

INDEX

INDEX

INDEX

INDEX

INDEX